W9-BVS-468

Preserving

Preserving

Putting Up the Season's Bounty

The Culinary Institute of America

Photographs by Ben Fink

ERICHO PUBLIC LIBRARY

HMH

This book is printed on acid-free paper. ∞

Copyright © 2013 by The Culinary Institute of America. All rights reserved.

Cover and interior photography copyright © 2013 by Ben Fink

The Culinary Institute of America
President   Dr. Tim Ryan '77
Provost   Mark Erickson '77
Senior Director, Educational Enterprises   Susan Cussen
Director of Publishing   Nathalie Fischer
Editorial Project Manager   Lisa Lahey '00
Editorial Assistant   Erin Jeanne McDowell '08

    For information about permission to reproduce selections from this book, write to Permissions, Houghton Mifflin Harcourt Publishing Company, 215 Park Avenue South, New York, New York 10003.
    www.hmhbooks.com

Library of Congress Cataloging-in-Publication Data
Preserving / Culinary Institute of America ; photographs by Ben Fink.
   p. cm.
 Includes bibliographical references and index.
 ISBN 978-0-470-90373-5 (cloth)
 1. Food–Preservation. I. Culinary Institute of America.
 TX601.P725 2013
 664'.028–dc23
                     2011035310
Printed in China
Design by Memo Productions, NY

TOP 10 9 8 7 6 5 4 3 2 1

CONTENTS

� � � � � � � � � � � � � � � �

HARVESTING AND PLANNING AHEAD

Preserving food takes time and planning, but the techniques are simple and the whole process pays off big. This chapter will give you the tools you need to plan your next project.

While times have changed since early preservation methods were developed, more people are preserving food than ever before. Why?

- ∗ Preserving food is economical. If you keep your own garden, preserving your own harvests is incredibly inexpensive. But even if you don't have a garden, preserving foods when they are in season drastically reduces your grocery bill—both immediately and later in the year.

- ∗ Preserving food is healthy. Home preserving means you are in control of what goes into your food — there are no additives, artificial colors, or preservatives. Most preservation methods do not affect food's nutritional value, meaning you can eat healthier foods year-round, even when they're out of season.

- ∗ Preserving food promotes locality, sustainability, and seasonality. Canning corn in the summer is not only good for your local farmer, but it also means that you won't be buying cans of corn shipped from miles away in the middle of winter.

- ∗ Most importantly, preserving food is delicious. Items that were originally created as a method of preserving food, such as pickles or smoked sausage, are now favorites because of their distinctive flavors. Preserving gives you tasty, fresh, healthy food year-round—which is something all home cooks can really sink their teeth into.

All of these benefits can be realized by following the techniques and recipes in this book. But in addition to learning how to preserve your own foods, you'll also discover methods for stocking your pantry, organizing your kitchen, and enjoying the bounty of the seasons more and more.

This can seem a little intimidating, but really, it's all incredibly simple. The techniques really work together. If you planned on canning 5 pounds of tomatoes but you ran out of time, never fear—you can freeze them instead! The processes you'll discover in this book have come from years of use and honing techniques—they can't all be done in one day. But if you begin following the techniques little by little in the ways that are most useful for you, you'll discover all the wonders preserving food has to offer.

SEASONALITY

In the early days of preserving techniques, cooks were limited to locally grown seasonal fruits and vegetables. With the modern increase in agricultural production and distribution, people are no longer limited to only what can be grown near them, and most large grocery stores and markets have certain items available year-round. While many people enjoy not being bound by the seasons when they shop, home preserving is the perfect opportunity to embrace seasonality.

For example, tomatoes are not available in the dead of winter, but you are hoping to make pasta sauce. You have several choices:

* You can buy fresh tomatoes from a large grocery store. They are out of season, so they are expensive and lacking in flavor.
* You can buy canned tomatoes, which may contain additional ingredients, including salt and preservatives.
* You can use the tomatoes you already have: canned, dried, or frozen.

The advantages to the last option are numerous, because buying food in season:

* is less expensive
* encourages and supports local markets and growers
* reduces your carbon footprint
* results in tastier, healthier food

GARDENING

While this isn't a book about gardening, many home preservers enjoy working with their own products. Gardening is even more rewarding when you get to enjoy the fruits (and vegetables) of your labor, and it's even better when you can do so year-round! It takes a lot of work to start your own garden, but here are some things to consider when creating a garden specifically with preserving in mind.

KEEP A BOOK WITH DETAILS TO MAKE FUTURE PLANTINGS MORE SUCCESSFUL. Keeping a gardening book is a useful tradition that will help you remember details from year to year. Keep track of the types of seeds you used, when they were planted, and when you harvested the final crops. You can also

Home gardens can be large or small, and they can be tailored to fit your personal preserving needs.

detail the amount each plant produced, its overall quality (flavor, texture, size), and whether you should grow more or less of the same product next year.

WHEN DO YOU NEED TO PLANT AND HARVEST?
Many seed packages have guidelines specifying how long they will take to sprout and grow to maturity. When your crop is ready for harvesting, you need to be ready to preserve it, so take note.

WHAT WILL GROW IN YOUR AREA? It's unrealistic to plant citrus trees if you live in a cold, rainy environment. Consider what grows best in your region to have the best chances of success.

PLANNING AHEAD

The best part about preserving food is that you can do as little or as much of it as you would like. Each year, you could make a huge batch of jam to use throughout the year and give as gifts. However, any good preserver has a plan. Things to consider:

WHAT DO YOU EAT MOST OFTEN? You will want to have more of what you like. Also consider how you will be using products. You may want to can some vegetables and freeze others, or puree some berries and leave others whole to freeze.

WHAT IS READILY AVAILABLE? If you live in an area with plentiful apple orchards, you may want to focus on preserving other fruit first, since it will be easier to get your hands on the apples later.

WHAT IS MOST AFFECTED BY SEASONALITY?
Consider items that significantly lose quality and/or increase in price when they're out of season. You may want to give those items priority.

WHAT IS AVAILABLE IN YOUR GARDEN, AND WHEN? If you're preserving items from your own garden, you'll want to be ready the moment they are ready to be harvested. In addition, you may want to plan your plantings a few weeks apart from one another, so that you don't have to harvest all of the products at once.

WHAT WILL YOU SUPPLEMENT FROM MARKETS AND FARMS? Do a little research to find out what crops are available from your local markets and farms—it will help you decide when and what you want to preserve.

HOW MUCH STORAGE SPACE DO YOU HAVE? Your storage space is valuable. Consider how you're going to preserve, and how much space you need to allot in your root cellar, pantry, or freezer.

CHOOSING THE RIGHT PRODUCTS

The key to any successful recipe is to choose quality ingredients. All foods have certain quality indicators that vary from product to product. Knowing what to look for can be helpful when trying to choose the best ingredients.

MEAT AND FISH Most types of meat are subject to a grading system, making it relatively simple to choose what will be best for any given recipe. Many small farms will not pay to have their meat graded, but they can identify and discuss the quality and/or types of meat available with you before you purchase.

BEEF Choose meat that is evenly marbled and red in color, and avoid gray or dry-looking meat. Beef is graded for both quality and yield. The three most common quality gradings available are **Prime**, **Choice**, and Select, with Prime being the highest quality grading. Yield grading is on a scale from one (leanest) to five (fattiest).

VEAL Choose meat that is light pink in color, and avoid gray or dry-looking meat. Choose Prime or Choice quality graded veal.

PORK Choose meat that is pink in color, and avoid gray or dry-looking meat. Pork is graded based on the thickness of the fat on the meat and on general size. While the layer of fat can be ideal for some recipes, it also increases the weight of the meat, so if you will be trimming it off, it's best to buy leaner cuts.

LAMB Choose meat that is evenly red in color, and avoid gray or dry-looking meat. Choose Prime or Choice graded lamb. Some markets will use the term *spring lamb* to reference a younger, smaller, and more tender product.

POULTRY Poultry is graded based on a number of factors, including the amount of meat compared to the bone, the quality of

---

CHOICE: A USDA grade of meat quality that has slight marbling.
PRIME: The highest grade of quality given to meat by the USDA.

the flesh, and the skin covering. Choose meat that is evenly colored, with no discoloration of the skin or flesh. It is especially important to handle and store poultry carefully to prevent contamination.

FISH   Choose fish that has a good overall appearance, with no bruising or cuts. The flesh should be firm and not overly soft. If the fish still has scales, they should adhere tightly to the skin, and the eyes should be clear, not foggy.

When purchasing live shellfish, look for signs of movement. Lobsters and crabs should move about. Clams, mussels, and oysters should be tightly closed, but as they age, they will begin to open, and should close when touched. Any shells that do not snap shut when touched should be discarded. Mollusk's shellfish should have a sweet and sea-like aroma.

DAIRY PRODUCTS   Dairy products are highly perishable, so it's important to inspect them before purchasing and use them relatively quickly. Milk, cream, and other dairy products are usually dated to give an indicator of their level of freshness and how quickly they need to be used. Be sure that dairy products are fresh before using them in any preserving recipes.

PRODUCE   Many grocery stores provide quality indicators on the signs for produce to help you choose the best product possible. Vendors at farmer's markets and farm stands are usually happy to discuss their products and help guide you to what you're looking for. Below are some guidelines for some commonly purchased produce.

CERTIFIED ORGANIC: Organic certification is a process that varies depending on the governing body and/or country. It involves standards of growing , storage, processing, packing, and shipping of food and other agricultural products.
COMMUNITY SUPPORTED AGRICULTURE: Also known as CSA; a community of individuals that supports a particular farm monetarily and/or through work. In return, the individuals receive the food produced by the farm.
HEIRLOOM: A cultivar of a plant that is not used in large-scale agriculture but was grown in earlier generations.

FARMERS' MARKETS

For those without a garden, your local market is the next best thing. Open-air and farmers' markets are some of the best places to start, since there are stands from multiple farms, all selling different items. But you don't have to stop there: Depending on your location, you may have access to a farm stand, a co-op, or a **community supported agriculture (CSA)** project. If so, you can buy a variety of fresh produce, dairy, and meat products year-round.

This ensures fresh product and also helps you support your local economy. You'll be surprised what local farmers and growers in your area have to offer—many are **certified organic**, raise local specialties, or have unique **heirloom** varieties for sale.

Farmers' markets are a great source for seasonal, local produce.

YOUR PANTRY: MAKING A STORAGE PLAN

Before you begin preserving food, it's a good idea to have a plan on how you're going to store your finished products. Each chapter in this book will have storage guidelines for specific items, but developing a basic storage plan can make things simpler and keep things organized.

Long, deep shelves are best for storing large amounts of cans and jars. Keep similar foods together (like jams, jellies, and marmalades on one shelf) to make them easier to locate. Label individual items and/or shelves to keep things neat and organized and to make sure you use products in the order in which they were made. For long-term storage of raw produce, you may want to consider building a root cellar or other cold-storage facility (see page 18).

The following chart gives an idea of how long some pantry staples might last when properly stored in your pantry (preserved items are in bold):

PRODUCT	APPROXIMATE STORAGE TIME
Canned foods	12 months
Dried fruit	6 months
Dried herbs	6 months
Dried vegetables	12 months
Honey	12 months
Jellies, jams, and preserves	12 months

Selecting Fresh Produce

PRODUCT	QUALITY INDICATORS	INDICATORS OF POOR QUALITY
Acorn squash	Sweet and fibrous flesh, heavy and firm	Cracking and soft spots
Apples	Heavy for size, good color, white or pale yellow flesh	Shriveling, washed out in color, pitted or soft brown bruising
Apricots	Plump, sweet smelling, with some softness to the flesh	Pale yellow in color, shriveling and hard
Artichokes	Firm and dense leaves	Dry, limp, under- or oversized stalk
Asparagus	Bright color and tightly closed tips	Shriveled, dry, or woody stalks
Avocados	Unblemished and heavy for size, uniform in texture	Soft spots
Bananas	Brightly colored	Black spots, pale-gray tinge to skin with no crushing at tips
Basil	Full bright color, vibrancy to the leaf, warm full aroma	Wilting, signs of deterioration, sagging stems and leaves, or off aroma
Bay leaf	Bright, fully green, glossy leaves	Bruising
Beets	Heavy for size, brightly colored	Discoloring, soft or saggy skin
Bell peppers	Good, solid color, bright sheen on the skin, thick walls	Multicolored skin, shriveling, soft spots, cracking or crooked
Blackberries	Plump, well-colored	Shriveling or signs of mold
Blueberries	Plump with deep, dark purple to blue-black in color	Red or green hues, shriveling or signs or mold
Boysenberries	Good color, plump, fragrant, and sweet	Shriveling, squashed or flat
Broccoli	Bright green color, tight florets	Woody stalks, yellow coloring
Butternut squash	Firm, heavy for size with more neck than bulbous seed end	Soft spots, greening, light weight
Cabbages	Even coloring, waxy surface, heavy for size	Blemishes, gray or white coloring

PRODUCT	QUALITY INDICATORS	INDICATORS OF POOR QUALITY
Cantaloupe	Tan to golden color below the netting, defined musky and sweet aroma, heavy for size	Green coloring
Carrots	Shiny, firm skin	Whitish color, molding, or cracking
Celery	Firm and heavy for size	Browning, bruised, or dry-looking stalks
Chayote	Light green, deep wrinkles	Sticky or discolored rind
Cherries	Plump, firm, richly colored	Shriveling, mold at the stems, brown or slimy stems, rock-hard
Chile peppers	Good, even color, warm peppery aroma	Soft spots, shriveling, signs of mold
Chives	Good color, pleasant onion-like aroma	Sliming, wilted or dehydrated stalks
Cilantro	Good, even-colored leaves	Wilted or exhibiting slime or mold, loss of distinctive aroma
Citrus	Heavy for size, firm skin	Blemished skin, signs of mold, soft spots
Cooking greens	Moist, brightly colored leaves and stems	Dryness, yellowing, or wilted edges
Corn	Heavy for size, plump kernels	Insect damage, dried kernels
Cranberries	Plump and brightly colored	Shriveling or pale in color
Cucumbers	Dark green color and heavy for size	Puckering, shriveled skin, or soft spots
Currants	Dry, plump, firm, and well-colored berries with a sweet tart flavor	Signs of decay
Dill	Light feathery fronds	Wilting
Dried legumes	Good color	Signs of dust or mold
Eggplant	Good, clean color and shine, heavy for size and firm	Soft spots or shriveling
Fennel	Firm, bright white bases and vibrant, crisp tops	Wilting, browning, or molding
Figs	Soft, fresh fruit with a clearly sweet aroma and stems that are intact	Dry, bruised appearance, or green

PRODUCT	QUALITY INDICATORS	INDICATORS OF POOR QUALITY
Gooseberries	Plump, evenly colored berries with a green stem, slightly tart in flavor	Molding or decay
Grapes	Good color, fruits firmly adhering to stem, green and pliable vine or stem	Pale or washed out in color, shrunken or shriveled, signs of mold where grape meets vine
Green beans	Dry product	Excess moisture
Honeydew	Larger and heavy for size, yellow to silvery-white rind	Smaller in size
Kiwi fruit	Firm but not rock-hard flesh	Shriveling, moldy areas, or bruising
Leaf lettuce	Moist, brightly colored leaves and short, dense stalk	Browning, wilting, or holes in the leaves
Lemongrass	Firm, heavy stalks	Signs of dehydration
Mangoes	Plump and rounded at the stem, clean and sweet aroma, heavy for size, good color	Shriveling
Marjoram	Bright and appetizing aroma	Wilting leaves or signs of slime or decay
Mint	Bright and fresh aroma, brightly colored leaves	Signs of deterioration, such as black, slimy leaves
Mushrooms	Dry and firm flesh and closed gills	Shriveled, damp, or slimy skin
Nectarines	Deep and vibrant color, firm texture	Greening
Okra	Brightly colored, firm-textured pods	Limp or pale pods
Onions	Shiny, tight skin and heavy for size	Sprouting, shriveled skin, or bruising
Oregano	Bright, vibrant leaves, with an assertive aroma	Wilting, signs of decay, or an off odor
Papaya	Fatty, textured flesh, juicy and smooth, warm yellow color in the skin, firm yield to pressure when squeezed	Stringiness, hard or shriveling, a fermented odor; gray tinge indicates chilling before fully ripe
Parsley	Solid and brightly colored frilly leaves, bright vegetable aroma	Decay, wilting, fading or slimy, sour aroma

PRODUCT	QUALITY INDICATORS	INDICATORS OF POOR QUALITY
Passion fruit	Heavy for its size and deeply colored	Decay
Peaches	Good color, distinct sweet smell	Green or dented fruit, bruising or shriveling, rock-hard
Pears	Fully matured and aromatic	Scuffing, pitting, bruising or shriveling in the skin or neck
Persimmon	Smooth, shiny skin with a full, bright color	Pale yellow patches, cracked, bruising or deeply scarred fruit
Pineapple	Plump, heavy fruit with some yield to pressure at the stem end, fresh green leaves, and bold color	Dull or browning leaves, or soft spots
Plantains	Large, heavy, and very firm	Shriveling or soft spots
Plums	Springy firmness to flesh, good rich color	Rock-hard flesh, shriveling and/or softening at the ends
Pomegranates	Hard-shelled, good color	Rock-hard, dull in color, shriveling, or cracked
Potatoes	Firm, smooth, and tight skin, little to no odor	Greening, sprouting, dark, or soft spots
Pumpkin	Heavy for size, stem intact	Green, cracked, or soft spots
Radishes	Bright color	Slimy tips, discolorations, or cracking
Raspberry	Plump, brightly colored berries with a hazy glow and sweet flavor	Wet, flattened, or shriveling
Rhubarb	Firm stalks that lie flat	Dry or cracked stalks
Rosemary	Firm and vibrant, distinctive aroma	Wilting, leaves with mold at the tips, a parched appearance
Sage	Good color, flat, vibrant leaves, and distinctive strong aroma	Curling or withered leaves
Shell beans	Plump beans	Mold, wilted, or discolored pod
Spaghetti squash	Bright yellow rind, heavy for size	Pale yellow, soft spots penetrating the rind
Star fruit	Firm and plump with good color	Shriveling or brown spots

PRODUCT	QUALITY INDICATORS	INDICATORS OF POOR QUALITY
Strawberries	Fully ripened and red berries	White shoulders, greening, wet or have dark or soft spots, and signs of mold at the stem
Tarragon	Vibrant, well-perfumed leaves	Withering or decay
Tomatoes	Firm, plump, well colored and sweet smelling	Cracking or soft, spongy spots
Thyme	Pale green leaves, bright aroma	Withering leaves, signs of mold, sour aroma
Watermelon	Healthy sheen on skin, dry and firm stem, heavy for size	Soft spotting, cracking, and bruising on the rind
Yellow squash	Bright color	Excessive bumping and pitting
Zucchini	Heavy, straight, firm with good color	Flabby, dimpled, or shriveled

SEASONAL PRODUCE AVAILABILITY

✽ ✽

The following charts list the produce available by season. Though these are an excellent guideline to seasonality, availability varies depending on your location. Those in very temperate places may be able to enjoy fresh produce year-round, whereas those living in places with harsher climates may have difficulty sourcing certain fruits or vegetables, or may only have them for a very short window of time. Also, many types of produce overlap and thus are available in more than one season.

SPRING

ARTICHOKES	LIMES	SNOW PEAS
ASPARAGUS	MANGOES	SORREL
BABY LETTUCES	MORELS	SPINACH
BROCCOLI	MUSHROOMS	STRAWBERRIES
CHIVES	MUSTARD GREENS	SWEET CORN
COLLARD GREENS	ORANGES	SWISS CHARD
FAVA BEANS	PEA PODS/SNAP PEAS	VIDALIA ONIONS
FENNEL	PEAS	WATERCRESS
FIDDLEHEAD FERNS	PINEAPPLE	
GREEN BEANS	RAMPS	
HONEYDEW	RHUBARB	

SUMMER

APRICOTS	GRAPEFRUIT	PLUMS
BEETS	GRAPES	RADISHES
BELL PEPPERS	GREEN BEANS	RASPBERRIES
BLACKBERRIES	HONEYDEW	STRAWBERRIES
BLUEBERRIES	KIWIS	SUMMER SQUASH
BOYSENBERRIES	LIMA BEANS	SWEET CORN
CANTALOUPE	LIMES	TOMATILLOS
CHERRIES	LOGANBERRIES	TOMATOES
CUCUMBERS	NECTARINES	WATERMELON
EGGPLANT	OKRA	ZUCCHINI
FIGS	PEACHES	
GARLIC	PEAS	

FALL

ACORN SQUASH	CRANBERRIES	PINEAPPLE
APPLES	DAIKON RADISH	POMEGRANATE
BELGIAN ENDIVE	GARLIC	PUMPKIN
BOK CHOY	GINGER	QUINCE
BROCCOLI	GRAPES	RUTABAGAS
BRUSSELS SPROUTS	GUAVA	SWEET POTATOES
BUTTERNUT SQUASH	HUCKLEBERRIES	SWISS CHARD
CAULIFLOWER	KUMQUATS	TURNIPS
CELERY ROOT	MUSHROOMS	WINTER SQUASH
CHAYOTE SQUASH	PARSNIPS	YAMS
CHERIMOYA	PEAR	
COCONUTS	PERSIMMONS	

WINTER

APPLES	KALE	RED CURRANTS
BELGIAN ENDIVE	LEEKS	RUTABAGAS
BOK CHOY	MUSHROOMS	SWEET POTATOES
BRUSSELS SPROUTS	ORANGES	TANGERINES
CHERIMOYA	PARSNIPS	TURNIPS
CHESTNUTS	PEARS	WINTER SQUASH
COCONUTS	PERSIMMONS	YAMS
DATES	PUMMELOS	
GRAPEFRUIT	RADICCHIO	

ROOT CELLARING

A root cellar is a storage environment specifically designed to store certain types of produce in a cool, dark place with controlled humidity levels. When all of these guidelines are met, a root cellar can be used to store foods in the winter with no fear of freezing. When the environment is particularly ideal, it can also increase the shelf life of foods.

Traditionally root cellars were built underground simply by digging a hole, perhaps into the side of a hill. Today, using the proper materials, cellars can also be built directly on the ground. The idea is that the soil of the ground is naturally cool and moist, providing the ideal conditions for a root cellar. A more modern and space-saving approach is to use part of a basement (especially an unfinished area). Even the staircase of a basement can work to store baskets of food as long as conditions are monitored.

Root cellars should be kept above 32°F and below 40°F. Humidity inside the cellar should be at least 80 percent. Foods that are commonly stored in root cellars include:

Apples	Potatoes
Beets	Pumpkin
Carrots	Rutabagas
Endive	Turnips
Onions	Winter Squash
Pears	

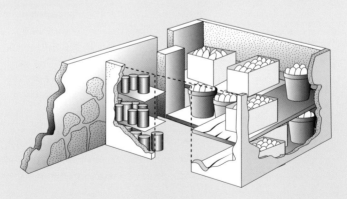

A root cellar can be as elaborate as a free-standing structure or as simple as a protected area of an unfinished basement.

HANDLING

XXXXXXXXXXXXXXXXXXXXXXXXXXXXXX

MEAT AND FISH   Meat and poultry should be wrapped and stored in the refrigerator. It's best to keep meat lower in your refrigerator, as it reduces any chances for cross contamination from dripping juices (this is especially important when handling poultry). Place wrapped meat on a baking sheet to make it easy to take in and out of the refrigerator (this will also catch any juices that may escape from the meat). Meat can also be frozen for longer storage.

Fish and seafood should be used as quickly as possible. It's best to store them on ice in the refrigerator. Frozen fish should be kept frozen until it's ready to be thawed and then immediately cooked.

DAIRY PRODUCTS   Dairy products need to be stored under refrigeration. Milk, cream, and butter should be kept away from foods with strong odors. Wrap cheeses tightly in plastic wrap to maintain moisture. Discard eggs with cracked or broken shells.

FRESH PRODUCE   Most produce should be stored under refrigeration. The exceptions to this rule are bananas, tomatoes, potatoes, and onions. Other guidelines to remember when storing your produce:

* Keep produce dry, as excess moisture can promote spoilage.
* Most produce should not be washed, trimmed, or peeled until just before use. Leafy tops on root vegetables, such as turnips, carrots, or beets, should be removed prior to storage because they promote moisture loss in the vegetable.
* Fruits that can ripen after being picked, such as avocados or peaches, should be stored at room temperature if they need further ripening. If not, they should be stored in the refrigerator.
* Some fruits emit **ethylene gas** as they sit in storage. This gas accelerates ripening and can also promote spoilage. Therefore, high-ethylene fruits (such as apples, bananas, and melons) are best stored separately, away from other produce.
* Some produce can give off strong odors (such as onions, garlic, lemons, and so forth) to surrounding items. Be conscious of this when storing these items. Likewise, some produce can pick up odors very easily (cherries and apples, for example) and should be stored away from anything potent.

ETHYLENE GAS: Accelerates ripening and can also promote spoilage. High-ethylene fruits include apples, bananas, and melons.

* Most items will begin to deteriorate after four to five days. Some items, like citrus fruits, root vegetables, and hard squashes, have a longer shelf life of up to two weeks.
* Herbs should be loosely wrapped in damp paper towels and refrigerated.

Food Safety

In any preserving technique, it is especially important to follow basic food safety and sanitation guidelines. Each chapter in this book will discuss the specific health and safety concerns associated with each preserving technique, but the following is a list of basic guidelines to follow in your kitchen to avoid food-borne illnesses, cross contamination, or spoilage.

CROSS CONTAMINATION   Cross contamination occurs when a harmful substance is transferred from one surface to another. The best way to prevent cross contamination is to be as sanitary as possible throughout preparation and cooking:
* Wash your hands frequently.
* Try to use separate work areas when working with varying food items like produce and meat products.
* Thoroughly wash and dry any storage containers, such as canning jars.

FOOD-BORNE ILLNESSES   Food-borne illnesses can be caused by chemical contaminants (such as cleaning products) or physical contaminants (such as glass) that accidentally find their way into prepared foods. The most common contaminants associated with preserving methods are biological contaminants, which include toxins and pathogens. Pathogens, such as fungi, viruses, parasites, and bacteria are the primary cause of food-borne illnesses.

Fungi (including mold and yeast) have a high tolerance for acidic conditions. Fungi cause food to spoil, but because you can see traces of the fungi directly on the food, most contaminated food is discarded before being consumed.
* Viruses do not multiply in food, but if they get on food due to contamination, they can cause illness. The best defense against viruses is to purchase fresh food and store it properly and safely.
* Parasites feed on other organisms. They can live in various types of food and, when consumed, they will continue to live

and grow. In some cases, they may lay eggs and multiply, all of which can be damaging and cause illness.

✳ Bacteria require three conditions for growth and reproduction: protein, lots of moisture, and a moderate pH (low acidity). If all of these conditions are present, bacteria can multiply rapidly. To protect food from bacteria, work quickly and cleanly, and avoid cross contamination.

TEMPERATURE DANGER ZONE   Bacteria and other pathogens are most comfortable in a warm environment between 41°F and 135°F. Below 41°F, food is properly chilled and spoilage and growth of pathogens are slowed. Above 135°F, food is being cooked and has reached a temperature where most pathogens are either destroyed or are unable to increase. If food spends any extended time (four hours or more) in the "danger zone," it may become unsafe.

This is especially important to remember when utilizing preserving techniques, as many processes will bring the food through this temperature range. Drying, for example, is done at moderate temperatures that can encourage the growth of pathogens. These foods should be closely monitored and timed so as to reduce any chance of contamination. Also, remember to follow correct storage instructions for preserved foods. Most foods will need to be kept in a cool, dry environment; see specific recipes for details.

PRESERVING IN SMALL BATCHES

Preserving is often viewed as a tedious task because it involves working with large batches of food to "stock up" a pantry or freezer. While preserving in large batches can be efficient in many ways, it is possible to preserve small batches of food as well.

Perhaps you get some late summer tomatoes or early fall apples, and you want to make a small amount of a single item. Just remember that the ratios for recipes in this book cannot always be simply reduced. Keep your eye on important ingredients like sugar, salt, pectin, **brines**, or cures to make sure that the recipes will work properly in a smaller batch. Follow food safety and storage guidelines to ensure safe, delicious results.

BRINE: A solution of salt, water, and seasonings, used to preserve or moisten foods.

PRESERVING

The term *preserving* is broad and can encompass many techniques. The following are techniques that are used in this chapter:

JAM Jams are made by cooking one or more fruits (or other produce) with sugar until they thicken to a spreadable consistency. The sugar acts as the primary preservative.

JELLY Unlike jam, jellies are made using only the juice of fruits or other produce. No whole fruit or pieces of fruit are used in jelly making.

MARMALADE Marmalade is essentially a jelly with the addition of pieces of fruit. In Orange Marmalade, for example (see recipe, page 37), pieces of citrus zest are included in the recipe, giving the finished product a different texture and a pungent flavor.

CONSERVE   Conserves are made with two or more fruits and often include nuts or dried fruits. The resulting texture is similar to jam — chunky but still spreadable.

WHOLE FOODS   Often referred to as "preserves," foods can be preserved whole. This versatile method can be used in many ways: Foods can be preserved in their own juices, in a syrup, or simply in water.

CONFIT   Traditionally, the term *confit* means food (usually meat) that is gently cooked and then preserved in its own fat. The term has now expanded to include other foods (namely citrus), which are cooked and preserved in their own juices. The result is tender and incredibly flavorful food.

INGREDIENTS

FRUIT AND VEGETABLES   Select produce that is fresh and ripe, but do not use overripe produce. Such produce can break down easily and affect the final flavor and texture of the preserved product. Wash and dry the fruit carefully, and trim away any spoiled, dark, or mushy parts of the fruit.

SUGAR   Sugar is vitally important to most of the methods in this chapter, as it is the primary preserving agent. It also adds delicious flavor and sweetness to preserved foods. Most recipes in this chapter use white granulated sugar, but brown sugar, corn syrup, and honey may also be used. Mild honeys that are light in color (clover, alfalfa, or orange blossom) nicely complement the natural flavors of most fruits.

ACID   Acid not only provides tart flavor to preserved foods but also aids in achieving the thick, spreadable texture of jellies, jams, and marmalades. Most recipes use citrus juice or vinegar to add acid to a product.

PECTIN   Pectin is a naturally occurring carbohydrate that, when added to foods, can cause them to thicken to a gel-like consistency. It is commonly used in various methods in this chapter to thicken jams, jellies, marmalades, and other products. Pectin can be purchased in most grocery or specialty stores in two forms: powdered and liquid. The two types of pectin are very different and cannot be substituted for one another. Powdered pectin is added at the beginning of a cooking technique, before the food is brought to a simmer. Liquid pectin, on the other hand, is added at the end of cooking.

Pectin also occurs naturally in many types of fruits and vegetables. Preserved products made with these foods usually do not need added pectin to thicken. Underripe produce actually contains more pectin that fully ripe or overripe fruit. Fruits and vegetables with a naturally high level of pectin are:

Apples	Cranberries
Bananas	Currants
Beans	Grapes
Blackberries	Plums
Carrots	Quince
Citrus	Squash
Citrus Peel	

REDUCING ADDED SUGAR IN JAMS, JELLIES, AND OTHER PRESERVES

In addition to being a sweetener, sugar has preserving powers—it helps keep jams and jellies fresh and tasty. Alternative sugars do not have these same preserving powers. However, there are a few ways to reduce or remove added sugar in recipes for jams and jellies. Some brands of pectin have been modified, and either include artificial sweeteners or can be used with artificial sweeteners. If you're using a modified pectin, follow the instructions carefully, as they may vary from any other basic recipe.

Another option is reduction. Bring fruits to a simmer and cook them for extended periods. This will reduce excess moisture and cause the mixture to thicken, resembling other preserves. In addition, some fruits are naturally very sweet. If these fruits have enough naturally occurring pectin, you can still create delicious preserves without adding sugar. These products, however, may have a shorter shelf life.

SALT, SPICES, AND OTHER SEASONINGS Many recipes in this chapter call for various seasonings to help amplify the flavor of the finished product. Salt, which can also be a preservative, is used in moderation in most methods in this chapter, and is added solely for a flavor boost. Herbs, spices, and other ingredients may also be added at various points during cooking.

EQUIPMENT

The right equipment makes canning much easier. While you can certainly preserve food without some of this equipment, the proper tools truly streamline the process.

JARS, LIDS, AND BANDS   Glass canning jars come in multiple shapes and sizes. They are made to hold up to the high heat of hot foods and lengthy processing times. Always use jars that are specifically meant for canning, as many glass containers will not form a proper seal and may not be able to withstand high heat.

TESTING FOR THICKNESS

There are few ways to tell if food has reached the **gelling point** and, therefore, the proper consistency. Some preserves will thicken as they cool, but can still look thin while cooking, so it can be difficult to tell if they are going to gel. Spreads that do not contain added pectin are often cooked to the gelling point—it is clear when they are thick enough because they are thick even when warm. For other products, the following tests are ideal:

FREEZER PLATE TEST: Place a plate in the freezer for a few minutes. Spoon a small amount of the warm product on the plate, and return it to the freezer for 1 minute. This process quickly cools the warm product and allows you to see whether it has reached the correct consistency. If it is not thickened enough, continue to cook. If it is gelled, the product is ready for canning.

SHEETING TEST: Dip a spoon into the warm product. Lift the spoon out of the product and watch as the product begins to fall. A properly gelled product will break away from the spoon in an even sheet as it falls. Products that are not yet ready will look thin and syrupy rather than thick and gelled.

When jelly begins to cook, it will be light and syrupy (left); as it continues to cook it will show signs of thickening (center); and finished jelly will drop in a sheet (right).

GELLING POINT: The point at which gelling occurs. For jams and jellies, it is the point when two drops form together and "sheet" off a spoon.

FERMENTING

Fermenting can be both a positive and a negative thing in preserving. Some recipes, such as kimchi or sauerkraut, use fermentation to build flavor in the finished dish. Salsas, chutneys, and other foods can also be fermented with very flavorful results. Food ferments best in large quantities. The process occurs because vegetables contain microbes that, when provided with the correct environment, start eating the naturally occurring sugars in the plant. As these sugars are consumed, acids and carbon dioxide release and begin to ferment the vegetables.

Use food-safe materials approved for fermentation, such as stone, food-safe plastic, or glass. Pack food tightly into your chosen container (a 1-gallon container can accommodate about 5 pounds of raw vegetables), and cover food with brine by at least 1 inch. Place a heavy, circular object (like a plate) on top of the food, and weigh it down to submerge it in the brine. This keeps the food tightly packed and fully submerged throughout fermentation time.

Other recipes, like pickles, when not properly executed, can result in accidental fermentation as the food begins to spoil. While many factors can lead to such spoilage, things you should keep an eye out for are overly soft, shriveled, or discolored food; a strong or bitter flavor; and/or scum or sediment appearing in the jar. All of these can be signs of fermentation, and foods with any of these issues should not be consumed.

Jars are sold with matching lids and bands for sealing. The bottom of the lid has a sealing compound that activates when heated during processing. The bands screw on to hold the lids in place. Due to the nature of the sealing compound, lids can only be used once; they will not form a seal a second time.

CANNERS   There are two main types of canners available: boiling-water canners and steam-pressure canners.

Boiling-water canners are pots (usually made of aluminum, stainless steel, or other food-safe metals) that are large enough to hold jars with plenty of room to cover with water. Canners generally come with a rack, which keeps the jars from directly touching the base of the canner. A lid is placed on the canner during processing to retain heat. They are relatively inexpensive, but you can create a makeshift boiling-water canner using items that are probably already in your kitchen. Use a large pot that is wide enough to hold multiple jars and tall enough that the jars will fit with room to attach the lid if necessary. To keep the jars from touching the base of the pot, place a circular rack in the base of the pot so that jars do not come in direct contact with too much heat.

Steam-pressure canners are also large enough to hold jars, but they are only held in enough water to constantly create steam (2 to 3 inches). These canners also include a rack to keep the jar from directly touching the base of the canner and to keep the steam circulating during processing time. The lid is a crucial part of these canners. It tightly clamps in place. It has a gauge attached that measures the level of pressure inside the canner. For specific instructions on use, carefully read the manual of any steam-pressure canner you purchase before using.

THERMOMETER   To make sure you reach the proper temperatures when precooking food for processing, use a thermometer. Any variety is fine, but long-stemmed or candy thermometers are an excellent way to get an accurate reading and keep your hands out of a steamy pot.

RULER   It's always ideal to keep a ruler on hand to aid in measuring headspace. It can also be used to keep your knife cuts similar in size so that your finished canned goods turn out perfectly.

JAR FUNNEL   These wide-mouth funnels are made specifically for canning, as they fit perfectly into the mouths of jars. A regular funnel will work in a pinch, but some foods will not fit through it, and it can teeter precariously during use since it is not made to fit the jars.

JAR LIFTER   This is essential for removing hot jars from a canner. They are wide and semicircular in shape so that they mold around the jar, making them more reliable than your regular kitchen tongs.

MAGNETIZED LID WAND   This small tool has a magnet on one end, which makes quick work of getting a hold of hot lids and bands.

BUBBLE REMOVER   This tool removes air bubbles, packing the food more tightly and ensuring the proper headspace in the jar. These can be purchased anywhere you find canning tools, but the handle of a wooden spoon or spatula or a chopstick works just as well.

Remove air bubbles from the jar, wipe off the edge and the lid, and check the seal to ensure a perfect finished product.

PRESERVING TECHNIQUES

PREPARING JARS FOR CANNING

Read over your recipe to determine what size and how many jars are needed. Be sure each jar has all three pieces (the jar itself, the lid, and the circular band that holds the lid in place) and that they fit properly. Do not use jars with noticeable imperfections such as cracks, chips, or bent lids and/or bands. Jars should be cleaned and heated before filling. This reduces the possibility of contamination from residue, dust, or other impurities being trapped in the jar. It also ensures that the jar doesn't break when it comes in contact with the sudden heat of cooked foods.

RAW PACK METHOD

This method is ideal for delicate foods that may break down too much if cooked both before and during processing. Food is packed into jars and hot liquid is poured over it; then the jars are sealed and processed. Wash and dry foods to be canned thoroughly. Pack the food into prepared jars, as tightly as possible without crushing the food. Bring the liquid to a boil and pour it over the food, leaving the appropriate amount of headspace. The combination of the hot liquid and the processing time will cook and soften the food inside the jar, which can cause some foods to shrink and rise to the surface of the jar. For this reason, it's especially important to pay attention to headspace in recipes that use the raw pack method.

HOT PACK METHOD

In the hot pack method, food is cooked prior to being canned. The food is usually cooked in the liquid it is to be canned in (syrups, brines, juices, and so forth), but some foods are simply cooked and then packed into jars, releasing their own juices in the packing process. This method is used for many reasons:

* It is the ideal technique for most foods, including produce and meat products.
* Cooked foods can be packed very tightly, which ensures a more accurate headspace and thus a better seal.
* Cooked foods require less processing time if being processed by the boiling-water canning method.

HEADSPACE

Headspace is the space left between the food and the top of the jar when canning. Recipes that call for canning throughout this book require that headspace be left between the food and the top of the jar. Headspace has multiple purposes. Some foods will expand as they are processed, so leaving room in the jar for that expansion is crucial to ensuring the jars are properly sealed. It is also important to leave headspace for the proper formation of a seal when canning at especially high temperatures (such as in steam-pressure canning). Below is a general guideline for headspace, but see specific recipes for recommended guidelines:

* ¼ inch for jams, jellies, marmalades, and so on
* ½ inch for tomatoes, fruits, or other foods high in acid
* 1 inch for low-acid foods or anything processed in steam-pressure canner

BOILING-WATER BATH CANNING

In this simple method, food is processed in boiling water. This process heats the food to high enough temperatures (215°F) to destroy bacteria and also heats the jars to form a proper seal.

1   Place the circular rack in the base of a large pot or boiling-water canner (be sure that the pot itself is no more than 2 or 3 inches wider than the burner on your stove). The rack keeps jars from directly touching the base of the pot, which could cause them to overheat or process unevenly.

Boiling-water canner should have a rack that fits inside the pot to keep the jars from touching the base during processing.

Transfer prepared jars to the canner, place the lid on top, and process for the required amount of time. If a seal is not formed, you may continue to process, although it may affect the texture of the finished product.

2   Fill the pot or canner with enough water to cover the jars, and bring the water to a rolling boil. Use tongs to place the jars on top of the rack, taking care to leave a small amount of space between each jar so that water can fully surround each jar.

3   Make sure the water covers the jars by at least 1 inch. Once the jars are inside, place the lid on the pot, and begin the processing time. Process the jars for the amount of time dictated by the recipe. You may need to add additional boiling water to keep the proper level of liquid for longer processing times.

4   Use tongs to carefully remove the jars from the water, and check to be sure a proper seal has formed. For a proper seal the center of the jars should be depressed and not give at all when pressed. Cool the jars to room temperature before tightening the rings on the lids and storing in a cool, dark place.

This method is used for foods that have a high level of acidity. The processing time will vary depending on the type of food, so refer to specific recipes for processing times. Some foods that should be processed with the boiling-water method:

Chutneys	Jellies
Curds	Juices
Fruit	Pickles
Jams	

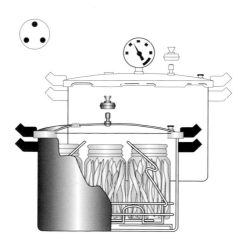

Pressure canners circulate steam around jars during processing. This method is used primarily for low-acid foods.

PRESSURE CANNING

Foods with less acid need to be heated to a higher temperature to properly destroy bacteria and other enzymes that can promote spoilage and food-borne illnesses. To reach this temperature, these foods must be processed in a pressure canner. Instead of coming in contact with hot water, the food and jars come in contact with steam, which can reach the appropriate temperature (140°F) and properly preserve the food.

1   Place the circular rack in the base of the pressure canner (be sure that the canner itself is no more than 2 or 3 inches wider than the burner on your stove). The rack keeps jars from directly touching the base of the pot, which could cause them to overheat or process unevenly.

2   Pour approximately 3 inches of water in the base of the canner. Bring the water to 140°F (unless a higher temperature is specified by the recipe). Place the jars on top of the rack, taking care to leave a small amount of space between each jar so that steam can fully circulate around each jar (See Headspace, page 29).

3   Place the lid onto the pressure canner and make sure it is secure. Remove the weight on the vent. Bring the water to a rolling boil so that steam flows freely from the vent. It is generally advised to let the steam release like this for at least 10 minutes.

4   Replace the weight on the vent and allow the canner to pressurize. When the recommended level of pressure has been reached (see the pressure gauge on the lid), processing time has begun.

STORING PRESERVED AND CANNED FOODS

Canned and processed, most preserved foods will safely keep for up to 1 year. Check the lids to make sure a proper seal has formed. The sealed jars should be rinsed to remove any food residue or other ingredients and thoroughly dried. Transfer the jars to a cool, dark place. If the temperature is too hot (75°F and above), it can speed the spoilage process. Likewise, if the temperature is too cold, the food may freeze, which causes many canned products to expand—breaking the jar or the seal on the lid. If the jars are exposed to too much light, it can alter the color and nutritional value of the food inside. Non-processed preserved foods, such as confit, can be safely kept refrigerated, but refer to specific recipes for recommended storage times.

5 Keep an eye on the heat so that the pot doesn't get too hot or create too much steam. Process tho jars for the amount of time dictated by the recipe. Use tongs to carefully remove the jars from the water, and check to be sure a proper seal has formed. Cool the jars to room temperature before storing in a cool, dark place.

This method is used for low-acid foods. Again, the processing time will depend on the type of food, so refer to specific recipes for precise processing times. Some examples of foods that should be processed with the pressure canning method:

Meat and poultry

Seafood

Vegetables

HOW TO PRESERVE AND CAN SAFELY

FOOD-BORNE ILLNESSES Food-borne illnesses, especially botulism, are common if food is canned improperly. Always follow proper canning procedures when processing foods to effectively destroy bacteria and other disease-causing enzymes. Test for proper seals after processing time, and process again if necessary. Store the jars in a cool, dark place. After jars have been opened, store them in the refrigerator to reduce chances of contamination. Discard any jars that contain food that is discolored or has visible mold.

SPOILAGE Always store processed foods in a cool, dry place. Overexposure to light promotes oxidation, which can cause food to discolor and can also destroy some of the food's nutritional value. Overexposure to heat can accelerate spoilage and reduce shelf life. Use a first-in, first-out system when opening and consuming canned foods: Label foods with the date that they were processed, and use older batches first so they are eaten before they spoil. All foods have differing shelf lives, so refer to the chart on page 10 for recommendations on how long processed food can be safely held.

CONTAMINATION Be sure jars, lids, bands, canners, and any other equipment used during the canning process are washed and dried carefully before they are used. Using clean equipment is the best way to prevent accidental contamination.

BOTULISM: A food-borne illness caused by toxins produced by the anaerobic bacterium *Clostridium botulinium*.

CONCORD GRAPE JELLY

This classic jelly can also be made with 4 cups of pure (no sugar added) Concord grape juice.

MAKES 4 PINTS

4 lb Concord grapes
½ cup water

7 cups sugar
1 packet (3 oz, about ⅓ cup) liquid pectin

1 In a large pot, crush the grapes with the back of a wooden spoon. Add the water and bring the mixture to a boil over medium-high heat.

2 Reduce the heat to medium-low and simmer, stirring occasionally, until the fruit breaks down, 10 to 15 minutes. Skim away any foam that rises to the surface as the fruit cooks.

3 Strain the mixture, reserving the juice and discarding the grape seeds and skins. Return the juice to the pot, and stir in the sugar. Bring the mixture to a boil.

4 Stir in the pectin and continue to simmer, stirring frequently, until the mixture thickens, 2 to 3 minutes more. Test the jelly for the proper texture (see page 25).

5 Pour the jelly into prepared pint jars, leaving ½ inch of headspace. Seal the jars, and process for 10 to 12 minutes (see page 29). Store in a cool, dark place.

STORAGE:

Processed, this jelly will keep for up to 1 year. Once jars have been opened, store them in the refrigerator, where they will keep for up to 2 months.

FIG JAM

This jam makes an excellent addition to a cheese plate. Alternatively, try it sandwiched between two cookies.

MAKES 4 PINTS

4½ lb figs, stemmed and coarsely chopped

5 cups sugar

¾ cup water

1 lemon, juiced and zested

Pinch of kosher salt

1   In a large pot, combine the figs, sugar, and water over medium-high heat. Bring the mixture to a boil.

2   Reduce the heat to medium-low and simmer, stirring occasionally, until the fruit begins to break down, 10 to 15 minutes. Skim away any foam that rises to the surface as the fruit cooks.

3   Reduce the heat to low and continue to simmer, stirring frequently, until the mixture thickens, 15 to 20 minutes more. Stir in the lemon juice, zest, and salt. Test the jam for the proper texture (see page 25).

4   Pour the jam into prepared pint jars, leaving ½ inch of headspace. Seal the jars and process for 10 to 12 minutes (see page 29). Store in a cool, dark place.

STORAGE:

Processed, this jam will keep for up to 1 year. Once jars have been opened, store them in the refrigerator, where they will keep for up to 2 months.

ORANGE MARMALADE

Orange marmalade has a sweet-and-sour flavor that is delightful with scones or other pastries.

MAKES 3 PINTS

2 cups thinly sliced orange peel	1½ cups water
1 lemon, thinly sliced	3 tbsp honey
3 cups orange juice	5 cups sugar

1   In a large pot, combine the orange peel, lemon slices, orange juice, and water and bring to a boil.

2   Reduce the heat to medium-low and simmer, stirring occasionally, until the peel becomes tender, 10 to 15 minutes. Skim away any foam that rises to the surface as it cooks.

3   Stir in the honey and sugar. Reduce the heat to low and continue to simmer, stirring frequently, until the mixture thickens, 30 to 40 minutes more.

4   Pour the marmalade into prepared pint jars, leaving ½ inch of headspace. Seal the jars and process for 10 to 12 minutes (see page 29). Store in a cool, dark place.

VARIATION:

SPICED ORANGE MARMALADE: Add 1 star anise pod, 1 cinnamon stick, 3 cloves, and 1 tsp ground nutmeg to the marmalade along with the honey and sugar. Remove the whole spices before canning.

STORAGE:

Processed, this marmalade will keep for up to 1 year. Once jars have been opened, store them in the refrigerator, where they will keep for up to 2 months.

PLUM JELLY

A classic, simple jelly that makes a great addition to baked goods or breakfast.

MAKES 4 PINTS

3½ lb plums

7 cups sugar

½ cup water

1 packet (3 oz, about ⅓ cup) liquid pectin

1   In a large pot, coarsely crush the plums with the back of a wooden spoon and remove the pits. Add the sugar and water, and bring the mixture to a boil over medium-high heat.

2   Reduce the heat to medium-low and simmer, stirring occasionally, until the fruit breaks down and the mixture reads 222°F on a thermometer. Skim away any foam that rises to the surface as the mixture cooks.

3   Add the pectin in a slow stream, stirring constantly. Continue to stir and cook for 1 minute, or until the mixture thickens. Test the jelly for the proper texture (see page 25).

4   Pour the jelly into prepared pint jars, leaving ½ inch of headspace. Seal the jars and process for 10 to 12 minutes (see page 29). Store in a cool, dark place.

VARIATION:

APPLE JELLY: Replace the plums with apples, and increase the water to 3 cups. Reduce the sugar to 3½ cups, and replace the pectin with 2 tbsp lemon juice.

STORAGE:

Processed, this jelly will keep for up to 1 year. Once jars have been opened, store them in the refrigerator, where they will keep for up to 2 months.

SOUR CHERRY JAM

Sour cherries make a delicious jam, but their season is relatively short. You may use frozen sour cherries instead; just be sure to thaw them completely and drain off the excess liquid before beginning the recipe.

MAKES 2 PINTS

7 cups pitted cherries, mashed slightly

3 cups sugar

Pinch of kosher salt

1 packet (3 oz, about ⅓ cup) liquid pectin

1   In a large pot, combine the cherries, sugar, and salt over medium-high heat. Bring the mixture to a boil.

2   Reduce the heat to medium-low and simmer, stirring occasionally, until the fruit begins to break down and the mixture reads 222°F on a thermometer, 30 to 40 minutes. Skim away any foam that rises to the surface as the fruit cooks.

3   Add the pectin in a slow stream, stirring constantly, and continue to simmer for 1 minute more, or until the mixture thickens. Test the jam for the proper texture (see page 25).

4   Pour the jam into prepared pint jars, leaving ½ inch of headspace. Seal the jars and process for 10 to 12 minutes (see page 29). Store in a cool, dark place.

STORAGE:
Processed, this jam will keep for up to 1 year. Once jars have been opened, store them in the refrigerator, where they will keep for up to 2 months.

JALAPEÑO JELLY

Seed the jalapeños based on how spicy you want the jelly. You can leave some seeds in for some extra kick, or remove all of them for a milder end result.

MAKES 4 PINTS

12 oz red or green fresh jalapeños, halved, seeded (see above), and chopped

2 cups apple cider vinegar

6 cups sugar

Pinch of kosher salt

1 packet (3 oz, about ⅓ cup) liquid pectin

1   In a blender or food processor, puree the jalapeños with 1 cup of the cider vinegar. Transfer the juice to a large pot.

2   Stir in the remaining vinegar, the sugar, and the salt. Bring the mixture to a simmer, and cook until it reads 222°F on a thermometer. Skim away any foam that rises to the surface as the mixture cooks.

3   Add the pectin in a slow stream, stirring constantly. Continue to stir and cook for 1 minute, or until the mixture thickens. Test the jelly for the proper texture (see page 25).

4   Pour the jelly into prepared pint jars, leaving ½ inch of headspace. Seal the jars and process for 10 to 12 minutes (see page 29). Store in a cool, dark place.

STORAGE:

Processed, this jelly will keep for up to 1 year. Once jars have been opened, store them in the refrigerator, where they will keep for up to 2 months.

BLUEBERRY-CURRANT CONSERVE

This conserve can also be made with fresh currants when they are in season by using 2 cups fresh instead of the dried currants and eliminating the rehydrating step.

MAKES ABOUT 3 PINTS

2½ cups water

1 cup dried currants

5 cups blueberries

3 cups sugar

1 tbsp lemon juice

1   In a small pot, bring 1 cup of the water to a simmer over medium heat. Pour the hot water over the currants and allow them to sit for 5 minutes, undisturbed, to rehydrate.

2   Transfer the currants and soaking water to a large pot over medium heat, and add the blueberries and remaining water. Bring the mixture to a boil.

3   Reduce the heat to low and simmer until the fruit breaks down, 8 to 10 minutes. Skim away any foam that rises to the surface as the fruit cooks.

4   Stir in the sugar and lemon juice.

5   Continue to simmer, stirring frequently, until the mixture thickens, 15 to 20 minutes more. Test the jam for the proper texture (see page 25).

6   Pour the jam into prepared pint jars, leaving ½ inch of headspace. Seal the jars and process for 10 to 12 minutes (see page 29). Store in a cool, dark place.

VARIATION:

STRAWBERRY-RHUBARB CONSERVE: Replace the blueberries with strawberries and the currants with 2 cups diced fresh rhubarb. Replace the water with 2 cups chopped oranges.

STORAGE:

Processed, this conserve will keep for up to 1 year. Once jars have been opened, store them in the refrigerator, where they will keep for up to 2 months.

RASPBERRY JAM

This jam recipe uses the naturally occurring pectin found in apples to thicken the jam—it's easy and turns out wonderfully every time!

MAKES 4 PINTS

9 cups raspberries

1 Granny Smith apple, peeled, cored, and coarsely chopped

5 cups sugar

Pinch of kosher salt

1   In a large pot, combine the raspberries, apple, sugar, and salt over medium-high heat. Bring the mixture to a boil.

2   Reduce the heat to medium-low and simmer, stirring occasionally, until the fruit begins to break down, 10 to 15 minutes. Skim away any foam that rises to the surface as the fruit cooks.

3   Reduce the heat to low and continue to simmer, stirring frequently, until the mixture thickens, 30 to 35 minutes more. Test the jam for the proper texture (see page 25).

4   Pour the jam into prepared pint jars, leaving ½ inch of headspace. Seal the jars and process for 10 to 12 minutes (see page 29). Store in a cool, dark place.

VARIATIONS:

STRAWBERRY JAM: Replace the raspberries with coarsely chopped strawberries. Increase the cooking time to 35 to 45 minutes.

MIXED BERRY JAM: A mixture of berries, such as blueberries, blackberries, strawberries, and so forth can be used in combination with or instead of the raspberries.

STORAGE:

Processed, this jam will keep for up to 1 year. Once jars have been opened, keep them in the refrigerator, where they will keep for up to 2 months.

CITRUS CONFIT

This can be made with any type of citrus: lemons, limes, oranges, grapefruit, and so on. Whatever type you choose, quarter the fruit. It will make it easier to remove the peel in one large piece, which is ideal for the confit process.

MAKES 7 CUPS

1 lb 13 oz citrus peels

3 cups sugar

2 cups corn syrup

2 cups water

1 Be sure the citrus peels are clean, and remove any excess pith. Too much pith will make the final product supremely bitter. Transfer the peels to a large pot and cover with cold water.

2 Blanch the peels by bringing the water to a boil, removing the pot from the heat, and draining. Repeat this step two more times with fresh water.

3 In a medium pot, bring the sugar, corn syrup, and water to a boil. Reduce the heat to low, and add the peels.

4 Simmer the peels in the syrup until they are tender and translucent, 1 to 1½ hours.

5 Remove the pot from the heat and allow the peels to cool to room temperature in the syrup. Transfer the peels and syrup to an airtight storage container and store in the refrigerator.

STORAGE:
The confit will keep, refrigerated in its syrup, for up to 1 month.

PRESERVED LEMONS

MAKES 1 QUART

6 lemons

Juice of 6 lemons

½ cup kosher salt

1 Wash the lemons very well. Cut each of the lemons into 6 wedges lengthwise and remove all the seeds. Place the lemon wedges in a very clean quart jar with a tight-fitting lid.

2 Add the salt and the lemon juice and mix well. Add more lemon juice if necessary to just cover the lemons.

3 Cover with the lid and refrigerate. Stir the lemons every day or two to help dissolve the salt more. Allow the lemons to "cure" for at least 1 week before using.

4 Store the lemons in the refrigerator. Rinse them under cold water before using.

STORAGE:

The lemons will keep in an airtight container, refrigerated, for up to 6 months.

STRAWBERRY SYRUP

The perfect topping for pancakes, French toast, or an ice cream sundae.

MAKES 3 PINTS

2½ qt strawberries, hulled and coarsely crushed

3 cups water

2 large strips lemon zest

2½ cups sugar

3½ cups corn syrup

2 tbsp lemon juice

1   In a medium pot, combine the berries with half of the water and the lemon zest and simmer for 5 minutes, skimming away any foam that rises to the surface as the mixture cooks.

2   Strain the mixture through a fine-mesh strainer lined with damp cheesecloth.

3   In another medium pot, bring the remaining water and the sugar to a boil over medium heat, stirring until the sugar dissolves. Boil until the temperature of the mixture reads 230°F on a candy thermometer.

4   Add the strawberry juice and corn syrup and continue boil for 5 minutes. Stir in the lemon juice.

5   Pour the hot syrup into prepared pint jars, leaving ½ inch of headspace. Seal the jars and process for 10 to 12 minutes (see page 29). Store in a cool, dark place.

VARIATIONS:
RASPBERRY SYRUP: Replace the strawberries with raspberries.
BLUEBERRY SYRUP: Replace the strawberries with blueberries.

STORAGE:
Processed, this syrup will keep for up to 6 months. Once jars have been opened, store them in the refrigerator, where they will keep for up to 1 month.

PEACHES IN SYRUP

Use firm, ripe peaches for this recipe. If you use softer peaches, you will need to reduce the cooking time to compensate for their tenderness.

MAKES 4 PINTS

6 cups sugar

6 cups water

4 lb peaches, halved and pitted

2 tbsp lemon juice

1 In a large pot, bring the sugar and water to a boil over medium heat.

2 Reduce the heat to low, add the peaches, and simmer until they begin to get tender, 12 to 15 minutes.

3 Raise the heat to medium, and continue to cook until the fruit is completely tender, 20 to 25 minutes more.

4 Remove the pot from the heat, stir in the lemon juice, and allow the peaches to cool to room temperature in the syrup. Cover and let sit overnight in a cool, dark place.

5 Pack the finished peaches into prepared pint jars, and cover with syrup, leaving ¼ inch of headspace. Seal the jars and process for 15 to 17 minutes. Store in a cool, dark place.

NOTES:

The same method can be used with raw fruit as well, such as stemmed, cored, and quartered pears or apples or stemmed berries. Pack fruit tightly into prepared jars, and pour boiling syrup over the fruit, leaving ½ inch of headspace. Seal the jars, and increase the processing time to 20 to 25 minutes.

Other flavorings can be added to the syrup, including vanilla beans, whole or ground spices, or citrus zest.

Syrup for packing is a mixture of sugar and water or juice extracted from some of the fruit. It should be heated just enough to dissolve all of the sugar. The syrup may vary in sweetness depending on your desired result. The amount of sugar in the syrup can vary anywhere from 10 to 50 percent of the total volume.

STORAGE:

Processed, this fruit will keep for up to 1 year. Once jars have been opened, keep them in the refrigerator, where they will keep for up to 1 month.

TOMATOES WITH GARLIC

This is a simple, classic way of preserving tomatoes that will allow you to have fresh, delicious tomatoes all year long!

MAKES 4 QUARTS

10 lb tomatoes, cored

12 garlic cloves, smashed

Lemon juice, as needed

1   Score the tomatoes with a paring knife, giving them a small X on the base of each tomato.

2   Bring a large pot of water to a boil. Add the tomatoes and blanch for 1 to 2 minutes until the skins begin to loosen.

3   Remove the tomatoes and shock them in a large bowl of ice water. Peel the tomatoes, discarding the skins.

4   Evenly distribute the smashed garlic between prepared quart jars. Pack the tomatoes into the jars. Gently smash the tomatoes as you add them to the jars, and they will release some of their own juices. Leave ¼ inch of headspace. Add 2 teaspoons of lemon juice to each jar.

5   Seal the jars and process for 60 minutes (see page 29). Store in a cool, dark place.

VARIATIONS:

TOMATOES WITH JALAPEÑOS AND GARLIC: Evenly distribute 10 seeded, thinly sliced fresh jalapeños among the jars as you pack the tomatoes.

HERBED TOMATOES WITH GARLIC: Add a few stems of thyme, oregano, or other herbs to the jars with the garlic.

STEWED TOMATOES: Slice or chop the tomatoes after blanching, and return them to the pot. Stew the tomatoes with 3 minced onions, 3 tbsp sugar, and herbs, if desired. Cook over low heat for 10 to 15 minutes before transferring to jars and processing.

STORAGE:

Processed, these tomatoes will keep for up to 6 months. Once jars have been opened, store them in the refrigerator, where they will keep for up to 2 weeks.

ONION MARMALADE

This savory marmalade is an ideal sandwich spread or condiment. Try it with sweet onions and champagne vinegar. We recommend storing this marmalade in smaller jars (½ pint or ¼ pint), as the intense flavor is best used sparingly.

MAKES ABOUT 2 CUPS

4 cups thinly sliced red onions

1 cup sugar

½ cup red wine vinegar

½ cup red wine

Kosher salt and freshly ground black pepper, as needed

1 Place the onions, sugar, vinegar, and wine in a medium pot over medium heat. Bring the mixture to a boil.

2 Reduce the heat to low, and simmer until the onions are tender and the marmalade has a syrupy consistency, 15 to 25 minutes. Season with salt and pepper.

3 Pour the marmalade into prepared ½-pint or ¼-pint jars, seal the jars and process for 8 to 10 minutes (see page 28). Store in a cool, dark place.

VARIATION:

ROASTED RED PEPPER MARMALADE. Replace 3 cups of the onions with peeled and diced roasted red peppers. Replace the red wine vinegar with balsamic vinegar and the red wine with white wine.

STORAGE:

Processed, this marmalade will keep for up to 6 months. Once the jars have been opened, store them in the refrigerator, where they will keep for up to 2 weeks.

SAUERKRAUT

If the sauerkraut is too liquidy at the end of 10 days, drain the cabbage and transfer the liquid to a large pot. Reduce the liquid over medium heat as necessary.

MAKES 2 QUARTS

6 lb green cabbage

8 oz kosher salt

1   Remove the outer leaves from the cabbage and cut the heads into quarters. Remove the cores of the cabbage.

2   Slice the cabbage into pieces about 2 inches long. In a large bowl, toss the cabbage with the salt until the salt is evenly dispersed.

3   Line a large bowl, bucket, or fermenting jar with cheesecloth. Place the salted cabbage into the bowl and cover with cheesecloth. Press the cabbage down to obtain a firm, even layer.

4   Weigh the cabbage down with plates, and cover the container loosely with plastic wrap.

5   Allow the sauerkraut to sit at room temperature for 10 days. Transfer the finished sauerkraut to storage containers and refrigerate until ready to use. Lightly rinse the sauerkraut before using to remove excess salt.

STORAGE:
The sauerkraut will keep in an airtight container, refrigerated, for up to 6 months.

TURNIP KRAUT

A different take on the traditional sauerkraut, this kraut can be used in all the same ways.

MAKES 1½ QUARTS

6¼ lb turnips, peeled and thinly sliced

¼ cup kosher salt

1 tbsp coriander seed, coarsely ground

1　In a large bowl, toss the turnips with the salt and coriander until evenly dispersed.

2　Line a large bowl, bucket, or fermenting jar with cheesecloth. Place the salted turnips into the container and cover with cheesecloth. Press the turnips down to obtain a firm, even layer.

3　Weigh the turnips down with plates, and cover the container loosely with plastic wrap.

4　Allow the turnip kraut to sit at room temperature for 5 to 6 days. At this point, remove the weights and cloth and make sure the turnips are fully submerged in the liquid they produce.

5　Continue to ferment for 5 weeks total, occasionally skimming the foam that appears on the surface of the kraut. The turnips will become slightly translucent. Transfer the finished turnip kraut to storage containers and refrigerate until ready to use. Lightly rinse the turnip kraut before using to remove excess salt.

STORAGE:

The turnip kraut will keep in an airtight container, refrigerated, for up to 6 months.

TOMATO JAM

This jam sounds like a savory treat, but it actually is quite sweet and makes an excellent accompaniment to pastries and pancakes.

MAKES 4 PINTS

8 lb tomatoes, coarsely chopped

⅓ cup packed light brown sugar

1 tbsp kosher salt

¼ cup apple cider vinegar

1 tbsp ground cinnamon

1½ tsp ground allspice

5 cloves

Pinch of freshly ground black pepper

1 In a large pot, combine the tomatoes, sugar, and salt over medium-high heat. Bring the mixture to a boil.

2 Reduce the heat to medium-low and simmer, stirring occasionally, until the tomatoes begin to break down, 10 to 15 minutes. Skim away any foam that rises to the surface as the fruit cooks.

3 Stir in the vinegar, cinnamon, allspice, cloves, and pepper. Reduce the heat to low and continue to simmer, stirring frequently, until the mixture thickens, 25 to 30 minutes more. Test the jam for the proper texture (see page 25).

4 Pour the jam into prepared pint jars, leaving ½ inch of headspace. Seal the jars and process for 10 to 12 minutes. Store in a cool, dark place.

VARIATION:

CARROT JAM: Replace the tomatoes with 4½ cups grated carrots, the brown sugar with 2 cups granulated sugar, and the vinegar with lemon juice.

STORAGE:

Processed, this jam will keep for up to 1 year. Once jars have been opened, store them in the refrigerator, where they will keep for up to 2 months.

KIMCHI

This technique may be applied to a variety of vegetables, such as radishes, turnips, cucumbers, daikon, and mustard greens.

MAKES 3 QUARTS

8 lb napa cabbage

4 oz kosher salt

1½ cups ground Korean red pepper

16 garlic cloves, coarsely chopped

2 tbsp minced ginger

½ cup mother juice (optional; see Note)

¼ cup sugar

16 scallions, cut ½ inch long

2 cups julienned daikon radish

1 Cut the cabbage into quarters. Spread open the cabbage leaves. Layer the leaves in a large colander, sprinkling with salt between each layer. Cover with a clean kitchen towel. Leave covered at room temperature for 2 to 3 hours. Squeeze out excess moisture.

3 In a food processor or blender, combine the ground red pepper, garlic, ginger, mother juice (if using), and sugar.

4 Coat the cabbage leaves inside and out with this paste. Add the scallions and daikon radish, and toss together to coat with the paste. Transfer the cabbage to a nonreactive container. Cover tightly with plastic wrap directly on the surface of the cabbage, and press down to submerge the cabbage in its juices.

5 Cover the container tightly with plastic wrap and let ferment at room temperature for 3 days.

6 Transfer the kimchi to the refrigerator and continue to age for 3 weeks (6 to 12 weeks will give you a stronger, very sour kimchi). If time is short, you may store the kimchi at low room temperature, 50° to 60°F, and it will ferment in about 5 days.

NOTE:
"Mother juice" is liquid from a previously fermented batch of kimchi that will help jump-start the fermentation process. If this is your first batch of kimchi, expect a slightly longer fermentation time. Be sure to reserve the juice for your next batch.

STORAGE:
Kimchi will keep, stored in a cool place in an airtight container, for up to 6 months.

PICKLING

Pickling is a traditional technique that preserves food by brining it or packing it in vinegar. The process tenderizes the food slightly, but the finished vegetables maintain a crisp texture and a characteristic sour flavor, and they have become a pantry staple.

INGREDIENTS

VEGETABLES Choose fresh, ripe vegetables for pickling. Avoid produce with spoilage, dark spots, or bruising. Overripe vegetables may become mushy when pickled. Wash and dry the vegetables carefully before beginning any preparation. Use the exact type of produce referenced in a recipe, as many items do not pickle well. Trim the ends off of vegetables, especially cucumbers. The end of a vegetable that was attached to the plant can contain various enzymes that can affect the texture of the finished pickled product and/or lead to spoilage. Be sure to use unwaxed produce—any produce with a wax coating will not properly pickle. Vegetables that pickle well include:

Artichokes	Celery	Onions
Asparagus	Cucumbers	Peppers
Beans	Garlic	Radishes
Beets	Ginger	Ramps
Carrots	Mushrooms	Zucchini
Cauliflower	Okra	

OTHER FOODS TO PICKLE

Vegetables are not the only foods that can be successfully pickled—many varieties of fruit make delicious pickles. Choose firm, ripe (but not overripe) fruits, as the pickling process will tenderize the flesh somewhat. You may want to pretreat the fruit (as you would for drying; see page 94) to prevent discoloration. Fruit is generally pickled using the raw pack method. Pack trimmed fruit tightly into prepared jars. Prepare the brine and pour it, hot, over the fruit, leaving ¼ inch of headspace. Seal the jars and process for 12 to 15 minutes. Fruit that is good for pickling includes:

Apples	Grapes	Rhubarb
Apricots	Melon	Tomatoes
Blueberries	Peaches	Watermelon Rind
Cherries	Pears	

In addition to fruit, other foods that can produce tasty pickles include:

Eggs
Fish and Seafood
Meat

VINEGAR AND WATER   Vinegar and water are the liquids used to make up the base of all pickling brines. Vinegar is also responsible for the distinctive tart flavor found in pickles. Most vinegars will pickle successfully, but distilled white vinegar is most commonly used because it will preserve the natural color of vegetables as well as maintain a basic, neutral flavor. Other vinegars that are used in this book include apple cider vinegar, champagne vinegar, rice wine vinegar, red wine vinegar, and white wine vinegar. Some of these vinegars may alter the color of the finished pickles. When preparing a brine, be sure to use filtered or distilled water.

SALT   Salt is one of the most important ingredients in any pickling recipe. It is used to flavor the brine and also acts as the primary preservative. In addition, salt is hygroscopic, which means it can often be used to remove excess moisture from produce so that the food's natural moisture doesn't dilute the brine during pickling. If the recipe includes this step, simply place food in a colander and sprinkle with salt. Toss to coat, and let sit until the moisture is removed.

SUGAR   Sugar is also a preservative, but it is usually added to pickling brines for flavor. It adds the balance needed to make pickles both sweet and sour. Most recipes use granulated sugar, but other sugars that can be added for alternate flavors include brown sugar, maple syrup, and honey.

SPICES AND HERBS   Spices and herbs are also used to flavor pickles. Most recipes call for Pickling Spice (see page 171), but feel free to use your own blend. For more flavor, toast whole spices before crushing them and adding them to jars. Always use whole spices—ground herbs and spices can darken pickles and/or cause spoilage. Alternatively, you may flavor the brine with a sachet made of whole spices or sprigs of herbs, and remove it before you pour the brine over the vegetables. Tasting the brine before you use it will allow you to adjust spices or other seasonings as necessary.

WATER   It is important not to use hard water for pickling. Hard water can darken the pickles, and a high presence of calcium or other minerals can adversely affect the pickling process. If your own tap water will not suffice, use filtered water.

Transfer prepared jars to the canner, place the lid on top, and process for the required amount of time. If a seal is not formed, you may continue to process, though it may affect the texture of the finished product.

EQUIPMENT

Since most pickles are processed, the technique requires the same equipment as other preservation methods (see Chapter 2, page

DISTILLED WATER: Water that has been purified by boiling and collecting the steam in a clean container.

25). The only specific concern is not to use utensils or supplies made with toxic metals (including copper, iron, brass, or galvanized metal), which can impart odd flavors and promote discoloration.

Remove air bubbles from the jar, wipe off the edge and the lid, and check the seal to ensure a perfect finished product.

CANNING FINISHING TOUCHES

These finishing touches are meant for any canned goods, not just pickles. Once jars have been filled, it's tempting to seal and process them right away. But a few extra steps will lead to a better end result. Take the time to complete these finishing touches for perfect canned goods:

REMOVE EXCESS AIR   Air bubbles naturally form in and around food in jars. Removing excess air bubbles will ensure a proper seal and that the headspace level is accurate. Canning supply stores sell a wand that can aid in the removal of excess air, but the handle of a spoon or spatula will work just as well. The method is the same no matter which tool you use: Simply dip the tool in and out of the jar anywhere you see air pockets.

CLEAN THE JARS   There may be a few drips or drops of food on the jar or on the outside rim. Take a moment to wipe off any mess from the jar—remnants can promote spoilage over time and/or prevent a proper seal from forming.

SEAL THE JARS PROPERLY   Place the lid carefully on the jar, and screw on the band tightly to ensure it fits well and will form an airtight seal.

PICKLING TECHNIQUES

FRESH OR RAW PACK PICKLING

Most recipes in this book use the fresh or raw pack pickling method. This method is generally used for pickles that are going to be heat processed. Food is packed into jars and hot liquid is poured over it, then the jars are sealed and processed. Wash and dry foods to be canned thoroughly. Pack the food into prepared jars, as tightly as possible without crushing the food. Prepare the brine by simmering vinegar, water, spices, and any other ingredients together. The combination of the hot liquid and the processing time will cook and soften the food inside the jar, which can cause some foods to shrink and rise to the surface of the jar. For this reason, it is especially important to pay attention to headspace in recipes that use the raw pack method. The jars can then be processed and stored. Most pickles made using the fresh pack method must sit for 2 to 5 weeks to allow the food to pickle properly and develop good flavor.

BRINING AND FERMENTING PICKLES

Most recipes in this chapter employ the simple fresh pack method. However, brining or fermenting pickles is also easy and can produce an equally flavorful pickle. This method is very traditional and slightly more time-consuming because pickles must sit in the brine for several weeks to allow the brine to penetrate and properly pickle the food.

To execute this technique, transfer washed and dried food to a food-safe pickling container (stone, plastic, or glass crocks are ideal). Pack the food tightly, and cover with brine by at least 1 inch. You can distribute spices or other seasonings by placing a layer on the bottom of the container and another on the top. Place a heavy, circular object (like a plate) on top of the food, and weigh it down to submerge it in the brine. This keeps the food tightly packed and fully submerged throughout the brining time. Skim any scum that rises to the surface each day. Most foods will need to brine or ferment for up to 6 weeks.

NOTE:
Many brined pickles may need to be desalted after brining is complete. Drain the pickles from their brine and cover them in cold water. Let the pickles sit for 24 hours, changing the water halfway through the soaking time.

BRINING: A means of preserving in which a food is either submerged in or injected with a wet cure.
FERMENTING: A process in which microbes in vegetables start eating the naturally occurring sugars in the plant. As these sugars are consumed, acids and carbon dioxide are released and begin fermenting the vegetables.

RELISH PICKLING

Pickled relish is a unique type of pickling in which vegetables and/or fruits are chopped and cooked in a flavorful brine. Simmering time will vary depending on the type of vegetables. Pack the hot relish into prepared jars and seal them. The jars can then be processed and stored.

STORING PICKLES

Processed, most pickles will keep safely for up to 1 year. The sealed jars should be rinsed to remove any residue of brine, seasonings, or other ingredients and thoroughly dried. Transfer the jars to a cool, dark place. If the temperature is too hot (75°F and above), it can speed the spoilage process. Likewise, if food is too cold, it may freeze, which causes many canned products to expand, which will break the jar or the seal on the lid. If the jars are exposed to too much light, it can alter the color and nutritional value of the food inside. Non-processed pickles, such as refrigerator pickles, can safely be kept for up to 1 month. If they are kept longer, they may be safe to eat, but they will generally suffer in quality, taste, and texture. Refer to specific recipes for recommended storage times.

HOW TO PICKLE SAFELY

There are several safety concerns to be aware of when pickling:

FOOD-BORNE ILLNESSES Food-borne illnesses, especially botulism, are common if food is pickled or canned improperly. It is especially important to follow proper canning procedures if you are processing your pickles. Test for proper seals after processing time, and reprocess if necessary. If you are not processing your pickles, be sure to keep them in the refrigerator in an airtight container. Discard any pickles that have become discolored, shriveled, moldy, or otherwise contaminated. In addition to following proper canning procedures, it is important not to alter the amounts of vinegar in recipes. Amounts of vinegar are crucial to maintaining the level of acidity in pickled foods, which prevents the growth of bacteria and other pathogens. Commonly used pickling vinegars (namely distilled white and cider vinegars) have an ideal level of acidity for pickling, but many specialty vinegars may not have an acceptable or known level of acidity. Without the proper levels of acid, foods will not pickle properly and the chances of bacterial growth are much higher.

SPOILAGE   An array of things can lead to spoilage in pickled products. To avoid spoilage, be sure to be careful during each step of the pickling process, using the following guidelines:

* Use good-quality, clean, and trimmed cucumbers and other produce. If food is spoiled, or has dark spots or other issues, it may spoil even if it is pickled and canned properly (sometimes pickles will even become hollow). This is also true for herbs, spices, and other flavoring ingredients. If they are not of the highest quality, they can contaminate the pickles.
* Use vinegars recommended for pickling (with at least 5 percent acidity). If a vinegar is not strong enough, food will not pickle properly, and this can cause the texture to change and reduce shelf life.
* Use salt that is recommended for canning or pickling. Many salts are iodized or contain other additives that can cause pickles to discolor, shrivel, or form a distasteful sediment in the jar.
* Use filtered or distilled water. Minerals found in tap water can cause pickles to discolor or take on off flavors.
* Use tools and equipment made of food-safe materials. Many metals (copper, brass, iron, and so forth) can give food an unpleasant flavor and cause pickles to shrivel and/or discolor.
* Process pickles for the appropriate amount of time and check the seals on each jar. Store pickles in a cool, dark place. Jars that are exposed to light or high heat are likely to spoil.

CANNING AT HIGH ALTITUDES

Altitude will affect processing time in canning. If you are 1,000 to 3,000 feet above sea level, increase processing time by 5 minutes. If you are 3,000 to 6,000 feet above sea level, increase processing time by 10 minutes. If you are 6,000 to 8,000 feet above sea level, increase processing time by 15 minutes, and if you are 8,000 to 10,000 feet above sea level, increase processing time by 20 minutes. These times are specifically for the boiling-water canning method. See page 62 for how altitude affects steam-pressure canning.

DILL PICKLES

Though this recipe includes processing instructions, these pickles can also be made using the basic brining method (see page 133). Just place the cucumbers, spices, and dill in a large bucket or other container and cover with brine. Be sure to use a weight to keep the cucumbers submerged in the brine.

MAKES 16 PINTS

¾ cup Pickling Spice (page 171)

3 bunches fresh dill

40 Kirby cucumbers, quartered

2 qt (8 cups) water

⅔ cup white vinegar

⅓ cup kosher salt

1   Distribute the pickling spice and dill among the prepared pint jars. Pack the cucumbers into the jars.

2   In a small pot, bring the water, vinegar, and salt to a simmer over medium-low heat until the salt is dissolved. Let cool to room temperature.

3   Pour the cooled brine over the cucumbers into the jars, leaving about ¼ inch of headspace. Seal the jars, and process the pickles for 12 to 15 minutes (see page 29). Store in a cool, dark place.

VARIATION:

GARLICKY DILL PICKLES: Add 2 or 3 smashed cloves of garlic to the jars with the pickling spice and dill.

STORAGE:

Processed, these pickles will keep for up to 6 months. Once jars have been opened, store them in the refrigerator, where they will keep for up to 1 month.

GIARDINIERA

✾ ✾

This tangy selection of mixed vegetables is a classic addition to any antipasto plate.

MAKES 4 PINTS

6 fresh serrano chile peppers, thinly sliced

1 red bell pepper, sliced

3 celery stalks, diced

2 carrots, diced

½ head cauliflower, stems removed and chopped into small florets

½ cup kosher salt

3 garlic cloves, smashed

2 tsp dried oregano

1 tsp red pepper flakes

½ tsp celery seed

Pinch of freshly ground black pepper

1 cup apple cider vinegar

1 cup olive oil

1   In a large bowl, toss together the serranos, bell pepper, celery, carrots, and cauliflower. Add the salt and toss to combine.

2   Pour enough water on top to cover the vegetables, cover with plastic wrap, and refrigerate overnight.

3   Drain the vegetables and rinse briefly. Pack the vegetables into prepared pint jars.

4   In a large bowl, combine the garlic, oregano, red pepper flakes, celery seed, black pepper, and vinegar. Slowly whisk in the olive oil.

5   Pour the brine over the vegetables in the jars, leaving ¼ inch of headspace. Seal the jars and process the giardiniera for 12 to 15 minutes (see page 29). Store in a cool, dark place.

STORAGE:

Processed, these pickles will keep for up to 6 months. Once jars have been opened, store them in the refrigerator, where they will keep for up to 1 month. The giardiniera can also be stored in the refrigerator, without processing, for up to 3 weeks.

PICKLED CELERY

Pickling really brings out the flavor in this usually mild vegetable. Pickled celery is a great addition to sandwiches, salads, and other dishes.

MAKES 2 QUARTS

1 bunch celery, trimmed

4 garlic cloves, smashed

1½ cups white vinegar

½ cup sugar

2 tbsp Pickling Spice (page 171)

1 tbsp kosher salt

1 Pack the celery into prepared quart jars. Distribute the garlic between the jars.

2 In a medium pot, bring the vinegar, sugar, pickling spice, and salt to a boil over high heat.

3 Pour the hot brine over the celery, leaving ½ inch of headspace. Seal the jars and process for 8 to 10 minutes (see page 29). Store in a cool, dark place.

STORAGE:

Processed, these pickles will keep for up to 6 months. Once jars have been opened, store them in the refrigerator, where they will keep for up to 1 month.

HALF-SOUR PICKLES

Sour and crisp, these pickles are perfect on the side of your favorite sandwich.

MAKES 7 PINTS

12 garlic cloves, smashed

3 sprigs fresh dill

25 pickling cucumbers, trimmed

1 qt water

2½ cups apple cider vinegar

3 tbsp Pickling Spice (page 171)

¼ cup kosher salt

1 Evenly distribute the garlic and dill and between prepared pint jars. Tightly pack the cucumbers into the jars.

2 In a medium pot, bring the water, vinegar, pickling spice, and salt to a boil over high heat.

3 Pour the hot brine over the cucumbers, leaving ¼ inch of headspace. Seal the jars, and allow the pickles to marinate, refrigerated, overnight or for up to 5 days before serving. Alternatively, the pickles can be processed for 8 to 10 minutes (see page 29). Store in a cool, dark place.

STORAGE:

Processed, these pickles will keep for up to 6 months. Once jars have been opened, store them in the refrigerator, where they will keep for up to 1 month.

PICKLED OKRA

✾ ✾

Crispy pickled okra is a delicious (and easy) way to enjoy this vegetable.

MAKES 4 PINTS

1½ lb okra

4 garlic cloves, crushed

3 cups white vinegar

3 cups water

½ cup kosher salt

2 tbsp dill seed, toasted and crushed

Cayenne pepper, as needed (optional)

1 Pack the okra tightly into prepared pint jars. Place a smashed clove of garlic in each jar.

2 In a large pot, bring the vinegar, water, salt, dill seed, and cayenne (if using) to a boil over high heat.

3 Pour the hot brine over the okra, leaving ¼ inch of headspace. Seal the jars and process for 8 to 10 minutes (see page 29). Store in a cool, dark place.

STORAGE:

Processed, these pickles will keep for up to 6 months. Once jars have been opened, store them in the refrigerator, where they will keep for up to 5 days.

PICKLED ASPARAGUS

The 4-inch spear measurement does not have to be exact — just be sure you cut the asparagus short enough so that it will fit in your chosen jar, with enough room for headspace.

MAKES 4 PINTS

3 lb asparagus

2 shallots, thinly sliced

2½ cups white wine vinegar

1 cup white vinegar

1 cup water

¼ cup sugar

1 tbsp kosher salt

1   Trim the asparagus to make spears about 4 inches long (see headnote). In a large bowl, toss the asparagus with the shallots.

2   Transfer the asparagus and shallots to prepared pint jars, packing the asparagus tightly.

3   In a medium pot, bring the vinegars, water, sugar, and salt to a boil over medium heat. Stir to make sure the sugar and salt dissolve.

4   Pour the hot pickling liquid over the asparagus, leaving about ½ inch of headspace at the top of each jar. Seal the jars and process for 12 to 15 minutes (see page 29). Store in a cool, dark place.

STORAGE:

Processed, these pickles will keep for up to 6 months. Once jars have been opened, store them in the refrigerator, where they will keep for up to 1 month.

PICKLED RAMPS

Ramps are in season for only a short time in the spring (between late April and early June), so buy them in bulk and preserve them while you can!

MAKES 2 QUARTS

2 lb ramps, trimmed

1½ cups white wine vinegar

½ cup water

¾ cup sugar

¼ cup Pickling Spice (page 171)

1 tbsp kosher salt

1 Blanch the ramps in a large pot of salted, boiling water for 20 to 30 seconds. Drain and rinse with cold water.

2 Pack the ramps tightly into prepared quart jars. In a medium pot, bring the vinegar, water, sugar, pickling spice, and salt to a boil over high heat.

3 Pour the hot brine over the ramps, leaving ¼ inch of head-space. Seal the jars and transfer to the refrigerator. Alternatively, you can process the jars for 8 to 10 minutes (see page 29). Store in a cool, dark place.

STORAGE:

Processed, these pickles will keep for up to 6 months. Once jars have been opened, store them in the refrigerator, where they will keep for up to 1 month.

PICKLED GINGER

The perfect accompaniment to sushi and other seafood dishes.

MAKES 2 QUARTS

1 lb ginger, peeled and thinly
   sliced

2 tbsp kosher salt

2 cups rice wine vinegar

¾ cup sugar

8 shiso leaves

1   Toss the ginger slices with 1 teaspoon of the salt. Let rest for 10 minutes.

2   Rinse the ginger in hot water and drain well.

3   In a small pot, bring the vinegar, sugar, shiso leaves, and remaining salt to a simmer over medium heat.

4   Add the ginger and simmer until it is tender, about 1 minute. Remove the pot from the heat and transfer the pickles to prepared quart jars.

5   Let the pickles marinate overnight before using.

STORAGE:

Store in the refrigerator, where they will keep for up to 1 month.

PICKLED EGGS

✠ ✠

This tasty snack doesn't have to be just a bar treat — these are easy to make for your own table.

MAKES 4 QUARTS

30 eggs

2 cups white vinegar

1¾ cups water

½ cup sugar

¼ cup Pickling Spice (page 171)

2 tbsp kosher salt

1   Place the eggs in a large pot with enough cool water to cover by at least 2 inches. Bring the water to a simmer, and cook the eggs for 12 to 13 minutes.

2   Drain the eggs, peel them, and transfer to prepared quart jars.

3   In a medium pot, bring the vinegar, water, sugar, pickling spice, and salt to a boil over high heat.

4   Pour the hot brine over the eggs and allow them to cool to room temperature. Allow to marinate for at least 24 hours in the refrigerator before serving.

STORAGE:

Store in the refrigerator, where they will keep for up to 5 days.

PICKLED GARLIC

Pickled garlic is a great addition to salads and sauces, and it is delicious all on its own.

MAKES 2 PINTS

4 heads garlic, peeled

1 cup rice wine vinegar

¼ cup white vinegar

2 tbsp Pickling Spice (page 171)

2 tsp sugar

1 tsp kosher salt

1 Pack the garlic tightly into prepared pint jars.

2 In a medium pot, bring the vinegars, pickling spice, sugar, and salt to a boil over high heat.

3 Pour the hot brine over the garlic, leaving ½ inch of headspace. Seal the jars and process for 8 to 10 minutes (see page 129). Store in a cool, dark place.

STORAGE:

Processed, these pickles will keep for up to 6 months. Once jars have been opened, store them in the refrigerator, where they will keep for up to 5 days.

PICKLED BEETS

If necessary, substitute 16 regular beets for the baby beets. After draining the beets, cut them into wedges or slices before pickling.

MAKES 2 QUARTS

32 baby beets, trimmed

2 red onions, thinly sliced

¼ cup sugar

1 tbsp kosher salt

1⅓ cups water

⅔ cup white vinegar

1   Place the beets in a large pot and add enough cool water to cover by at least 2 inches. Bring to a boil over medium heat.
2   Reduce heat to low and simmer until the beets are just tender, about 15 minutes. Drain the beets, and rinse with cool water. When the beets are cool enough to handle, peel them and set them aside in a large bowl.
3   In a medium pot, combine the onions, sugar, salt, water, and vinegar. Bring the mixture to a boil over medium heat. Reduce the heat to low and simmer for 5 minutes.
4   Pour the brine over the beets and allow the mixture to cool to room temperature.
5   Transfer the pickles to storage containers and allow to marinate overnight before serving.

STORAGE:

Processed, these pickles will keep for up to 6 months. Once jars have been opened, store them in the refrigerator, where they will keep for up to 5 days.

PICKLED JALAPEÑOS

You can substitute other hot chile peppers, such as habaneros, for the jalapeños.

MAKES 2 PINTS

8 oz fresh jalapeños, seeded and thinly sliced

2 garlic cloves, smashed

1 cup apple cider vinegar

¼ cup water

1 tbsp honey

1 tbsp Pickling Spice (page 171)

2 tsp kosher salt

1   Pack the peppers tightly into prepared pint jars. Place a smashed clove of garlic in each jar.

2   In a medium pot, bring the vinegar, water, honey, pickling spice, and salt to a boil.

3   Pour the hot brine over the jalapeños, leaving ½ inch of headspace. Seal the jars and process for 12 to 15 minutes (see page 29). Store in a cool, dark place.

STORAGE:
Processed, these pickles will keep for up to 6 months. Once jars have been opened, store them in the refrigerator, where they will keep for up to 1 month.

PEACH PICKLES

These sweet-and-sour pickles go well with bitter salad greens and cheese, as well as with chicken and pork.

MAKES 3 QUARTS

8 lb peaches

Fresh lemon juice, as needed

4 cinnamon sticks

2 tbsp cloves

1 tbsp peeled and grated fresh ginger

6 cups sugar

1 qt white vinegar

1   Blanche, peel, halve, and pit the peaches and hold them in water that is lightly acidulated with lemon juice to prevent browning.

2   Tie the cinnamon, cloves, and ginger into a small piece of cheesecloth to make a sachet. Bring the sachet, sugar, and vinegar to a boil in a large pot. Reduce the heat to low and simmer the brine for 5 minutes.

3   Add the peaches and cook until they begin to tenderize, 6 to 8 minutes. Remove the pot from the heat and let it stand in a cool, dark place for 24 hours.

4   Pack the peaches into prepared quart jars. Bring the brine back to a simmer, and remove the sachet.

5   Pour the hot brine over the peaches, leaving ½ inch of headspace. Seal the jars and process for 15 to 17 minutes (see page 29). Store in a cool, dark place.

STORAGE:

Processed, these pickles will keep for up to 6 months. Once jars have been opened, store them in the refrigerator, where they will keep for up to 1 month.

PICKLED GREEN BEANS

Green beans make excellent, crisp pickles that are great for snacking or as an addition to a relish tray.

MAKES 4 PINTS

4 garlic cloves, smashed

½ cup Pickling Spice (page 171)

2 tsp red pepper flakes

2 lb green beans, trimmed

2 cups white vinegar

1 cup water

¼ cup kosher salt

1   Evenly distribute the garlic, pickling spice, and red pepper flakes among prepared pint jars.

2   Pack the beans tightly into the jars.

3   In a small pot, bring the vinegar, water, and salt to a boil over medium heat.

4   Pour the hot brine over the beans, leaving ¼ inch headspace. Seal the jars and process for 8 to 10 minutes (see page 29). Store the pickles for at least 2 weeks before opening for maximum flavor development.

VARIATION:

DILLY BEANS: Evenly distribute 2 bunches of dill among the jars along with the pickling spice and red pepper flakes.

STORAGE:

Processed, these pickles will keep for up to 6 months. Once jars have been opened, store them in the refrigerator, where they will keep for up to 5 days.

PICKLED CUCUMBER SALAD

This simple salad can be used as a side dish, a salad topping, or a garnish.

MAKES 2 QUARTS

8 cups thinly sliced European cucumbers

1 cup thinly sliced onions

1 tbsp kosher salt

½ cup white vinegar

⅓ cup sugar

1 In a medium bowl, toss together the cucumbers, onions, and salt. Let stand at room temperature for 2 hours. Rinse the mixture and drain well.

2 In a medium pot, bring the vinegar and sugar to a simmer. Simmer, stirring occasionally, until the sugar is completely dissolved. Allow to cool completely.

3 Pour the cooled vinegar mixture over the cucumbers and onions. Transfer the salad to storage containers and let marinate in the refrigerator for 3 days before serving.

STORAGE:

Store in the refrigerator, where it will keep for up to 1 month.

SWEET PICKLE CHIPS

Be sure to cut your cucumbers and onions evenly so that they all have the same texture when they finish pickling.

MAKES 3 QUARTS

4 lb European cucumbers, sliced ¼ inch thick

1 lb onions, sliced ¼ inch thick

2 qts water

3 cups apple cider vinegar

1 tbsp kosher salt

2 tsp mustard seed

4 cups sugar

2½ cups white vinegar

2 tbsp celery seed

1 tbsp allspice berries, crushed

2 tsp ground turmeric

1   In a large pot, combine the cucumbers, onions, water, cider vinegar, salt, mustard seeds, and 2 tablespoons of the sugar. Bring the mixture to a simmer and cook for 10 minutes.

2   Drain the cucumbers and onions, and discard the liquid. Transfer the cucumbers and onions to a large bowl.

3   In a medium pot, bring the remaining sugar and the white vinegar, celery seed, allspice, and turmeric to a boil over high heat.

4   Pour the hot liquid over the cucumbers and onions. Transfer the pickles to storage containers and let marinate in the refrigerator for 3 days before serving.

STORAGE:
Store in the refrigerator, where it will keeps for up to 1 month.

Pickle Relish

Soy Pickles

Pickle Cucumber Salad

PICKLE RELISH

Other vegetables also make excellent relishes—try tomatoes or corn!

MAKES 6 PINTS

5 Kirby cucumbers, seeded and chopped

2 red bell peppers, chopped

2 green bell peppers, chopped

1 onion, chopped

½ cup Kosher salt

1½ qt (6 cups) warm water

1 qt (4 cups) white vinegar

1½ cups light brown sugar

½ cup Pickling Spice (page 171)

1 tbsp ground turmeric

1 In a large bowl, combine the cucumbers, peppers, and onion. In a large pot, stir the salt into the warm water until it is dissolved.

2 Pour the salted water over the vegetables. Cover and let the mixture sit for 2 hours. Drain the vegetables and rinse thoroughly in cold water.

3 In a large pot, bring the vinegar, sugar, pickling spice, and turmeric to a boil over high heat. Remove the pot from the heat, and add the vegetables.

4 Cover the pot and let rest overnight (8 to 10 hours). Return the pot to the stove, and bring the mixture to a boil.

5 Pack the hot relish into prepared pint jars, leaving ⅛ inch of headspace. Seal the jars and process for 10 to 12 minutes (see page 29). Store in a cool, dark place.

STORAGE:

Processed, this relish will keep for up to 6 months. Once jars have been opened, store them in the refrigerator, where they will keep for up to 1 month.

SOY PICKLES

This mixture of pickled vegetables makes an excellent garnish or salad on the side of Asian foods.

MAKES 2 QUARTS

3 cups soy sauce

2 cups rice wine vinegar

1 cup water

2 cups sugar

Korean ground red pepper, as needed

7 cups sliced European cucumbers

4 cups sliced daikon radishes

2 cups sliced red bell peppers

1 cup sliced carrots

1   Bring the soy sauce, vinegar, water, and sugar to a simmer over medium heat. Simmer until the sugar is completely dissolved. Stir in the Korean red pepper powder.

2   In a large bowl, toss together the cucumber, daikon, bell peppers, and carrot.

3   Pour the finished brine over the vegetables. Toss to combine.

4   Transfer the finished mixture to storage containers. Let marinate, refrigerated, for 3 days before serving.

STORAGE:
Store in the refrigerator, where they will keep for up to 2 weeks.

ZUCCHINI PICKLES

❋ ❋

These pickles are a nice variation on the classic cucumber variety.

MAKES 4 PINTS

4 lb zucchini, sliced ¼ inch thick

1 onion, thinly sliced

½ cup kosher salt

1½ qt white vinegar

4 cups sugar

4 tsp mustard seed

4 tsp celery seed

4 tsp ground turmeric

1   In a large bowl, toss the zucchini, onion, and salt to combine.

2   Let the mixture sit for 2 hours. Drain the vegetables, rinse them lightly, and drain again.

3   Transfer the vegetables to the prepared pint jars, packing them tightly.

4   In a medium pot, bring the vinegar, sugar, mustard seed, celery seed, and turmeric to a boil over medium heat. Stir to make sure the sugar dissolves.

5   Pour the hot pickling liquid over the zucchini, leaving about ½ inch of headspace. Seal the jars and process for 12 to 15 minutes (see page 29). Store in a cool, dark place.

STORAGE:

Processed, these pickles will keep for 6 months. Once opened, they should be stored in the refrigerator, where they will keep for up to 1 month.

COCKTAIL ONIONS

Making your own cocktail onions will add a touch of sophistication to your home bar and your favorite martini.

MAKES 2 PINTS

2 lb pearl onions, peeled

3 cups white vinegar

½ cup sugar

3 tbsp Pickling Spice (page 171)

1 tbsp kosher salt

2 tsp red pepper flakes

1 Pack the onions into prepared pint jars.

2 In a medium pot, bring the vinegar, sugar, pickling spice, salt, and red pepper flakes to a boil over high heat.

3 Pour the hot brine over the onions, leaving ¼ inch of headspace. Seal the jars and process for 8 to 10 minutes (see page 29). Store in a cool, dark place.

VARIATION:

PICKLED RED ONIONS: Substitute 2 thinly sliced red onions for the pearl onions. These onions should be stored in the refrigerator, where they will keep for up to 1 month.

STORAGE:

Processed, these will keep for up to 6 months. Once jars have been opened, store them in the refrigerator, where they will keep for up to 1 month.

SWEET PICKLED PEPPERS

✺ ✺

Any kind of sweet peppers will work for this recipe, but red bell peppers and peppadews work especially well.

MAKES 2 QUARTS

8 cups trimmed and sliced
   (if necessary) sweet peppers

1¾ cups white wine vinegar

¾ cup water

2 cups sugar

¼ cup Pickling Spice (page 171)

1 tbsp kosher salt

1   Pack the peppers tightly into prepared quart jars.

2   In a medium pot, bring the vinegar, water, sugar, pickling spice, and salt to a boil over high heat.

3   Pour the hot brine over the peppers, leaving ¼ inch of headspace. Seal the jars and transfer to the refrigerator. Allow to rest for 8 to 10 hours before serving, for best results. Alternatively, the jars may be processed for 8 to 10 minutes (see page 29) and stored in a cool, dark place.

STORAGE:

Processed, these pickles will keep for up to 6 months. Once jars have been opened, store them in the refrigerator, where they will keep for up to 1 month.

DRYING AND DEHYDRATING

Drying foods is a simple way to preserve them. In most cases, drying retains the nutritional content of foods, concentrates their flavors, and extends their shelf life. There are several methods of drying, most of which require no specialized equipment.There are several things to consider when drying or dehydrating food. First and foremost is the type of food being dried. Produce, for example, should be at its ripest to dry quickly and efficiently. However, many types of produce can discolor during dehydration, unless they are pretreated (see page 94). Also consider the size of the food. Certain foods can be dried whole, such as apricots or chile peppers, while others need to be halved or quartered. The final use of the food is important as well — some foods are dried as both a method of preservation and a way to ease storage of the food. Dried mushrooms, for example, have a long shelf life and take up very little storage space, but they must be carefully rehydrated before use. Dried fruit, on the other hand, maintains some level of moisture even after drying, which gives it its signature chewy texture. All of these factors play an important role in how the food is dried. Always consider them when choosing a technique to use to dry food, to help you understand how the food should be handled before, during, and after drying.

FRUIT

Fruit to be dried should be very ripe. Wash and dry the fruit well; don't soak the fruit, simply rinse it to remove any impurities. Too much time in the water will cause some fruit to absorb additional moisture and become soggy and difficult to dry. Because fruit is delicate and some varieties can oxidize quickly, it's important to prepare only as much fruit as you can dry in one batch. To prevent oxidation, you can keep the fruits in acidulated water (2 tablespoons of lemon juice in a quart of cool water) until ready to dry, but only for 15 minutes or less, or the fruit may begin to absorb excess water. Trim the fruit to the proper size, taking care to remove any overripe spots or bruises. Fruits that dry particularly well include:

Apples	Cranberries	Papaya
Apricots	Currants	Peaches
Bananas	Dates	Pears
Blueberries	Figs	Persimmons
Cherries	Grapes	Pineapple
Citrus Fruits	Kiwi	Plums
Coconut	Melon	

PRETREATING

Fruit is often pretreated before drying. Pretreating prevents oxidization so that food maintains its color and also keeps more of the nutrients in the fruit. Pretreating is not necessary, but fruits that are not pretreated will oxidize during drying and should be stored in the refrigerator or freezer to extend their shelf life. There are several ways to pretreat:

STEAMING   This method doesn't work for all fruit, because some will not hold up for the duration of the steaming. It can also affect the flavor and texture of the fruit drastically and result in a less desirable dried product. Place prepared fruit in a steamer tray, cover, and steam until the fruit is heated through (but do not steam so long that the process cooks the fruit). Transfer the steamed fruit to drying trays.

SYRUP BLANCHING   Some fruit will deteriorate before it can be properly blanched and therefore should not be pretreated with this method (primarily delicate fruits, such as berries or citrus). Make a simple syrup by bringing 2 cups sugar and 2 cups water to a boil over medium heat. This will make 1 quart of blanching syrup, which will accommodate 1½ pounds of fruit. Add the fruit to the simmering syrup and blanch for 5 minutes. Remove the pot from the heat and let the fruit cool in the syrup until it reaches room temperature, 25 to 30 minutes. Drain the fruit, rinse it lightly, and transfer to drying trays.

FRUIT LEATHER

Fruit leather, pureed fruit that is dried in sheets, is one of the most popular ways to enjoy dried fruit. It's very simple to make. Most recipes require fruit to be cooked until it becomes soft (though you can also use frozen or canned fruit for most recipes). After cooking, fruit is pureed until smooth. Lemon juice, **ascorbic acid** (which can be purchased in grocery stores or drugstores), or another acid should be added to help the fruit maintain its color. Line a baking sheet with a silicone mat. Pour the fruit mixture onto the prepared pan and spread it in an even layer about ¼ inch thick. The fruit can now be dried in a dehydrator or in the oven. When it's fully dry, remove it from the pan and cut into the desired size. You can dust it with cornstarch to prevent it from sticking to anything, or wrap it in waxed paper for longer-term storage. Keep the finished fruit leather stored in an airtight container.

ASCORBIC ACID   Ascorbic acid can be purchased from grocery stores, drugstores, specialty food stores, and preserving suppliers. Pretreating with ascorbic acid is not as effective or as long-lasting as sulfiting or sulfuring. Mix 2 tsp ascorbic acid with 1 quart of water in a large bowl. Add the fruit and soak for 5 minutes. Drain, and transfer to drying trays.

SULFITING   Sodium bisulfite can be purchased from grocery stores, drugstores, or preserving suppliers. Sulfiting will extend drying time slightly, but it is an effective method of pretreating. Mix 2 tbsp sodium bisulfite into 1 gallon of water in a large bowl. Add the fruit and soak for 5 minutes. Drain, rinse it lightly, and transfer to drying trays.

STORING DRIED FRUITS

Dried fruits should be stored in an airtight container in a dark, dry, cool place. If properly pretreated and dried, most fruits will keep for 2 to 3 weeks. Keeping dried fruits in the refrigerator or freezer will extend their shelf life. Refrigerated dried fruits will last for 3 to 5 weeks, while frozen dried fruit may be safely stored for up to 2 months. If the fruit shows any visible molding, discoloration, or shriveling, discard it.

SULFURING

Sulfuring is the most effective, longest-lasting pretreating technique. However, it is also more complex (It requires special equipment) and time-consuming than other techniques. Because sulfur fumes can be harmful, sulfuring should be done outdoors in a prepared sulfuring box. Fruit should be placed on a tray (the same as any drying tray), then on a rack where it will be suspended. Place the sulfur in a metal dish, light it, and cover the whole setup with a box (preferably with vents). Leave the fruit to absorb the fumes for 10 minutes, then close the box's vents and leave for 1 hour. Fruit that has been sulfured cannot be oven-dried. Sulfur can be purchased at grocery stores, drugstores, or preserving suppliers.

ASCORBIC ACID: Another name for vitamin C, which is found in citrus fruits. It is available in powdered or tablet form. It may be used to prevent fruit from browning.

VEGETABLES

XXXXXXXXXXXXXXXXXXXXXXXXXXXXXXXXXX

Vegetables do not respond as well to drying as other foods. Be sure to use very fresh vegetables, because fresh-picked vegetables dry faster and produce a higher-quality finished product. Wash and dry vegetables carefully, and trim them as needed. Below is a list of vegetables recommended for drying (tomatoes are actually fruit, but they do not require pretreatment, so they are listed with vegetables):

Beets	Horseradish	Peas
Cabbage	Legumes	Peppers
Carrots	Lima Beans	Potatoes
Corn	Mushrooms	Sweet Potatoes
Cucumbers	Okra	Tomatoes
Garlic	Onions	Turnips
Green Beans	Parsnips	

PRETREATING   Many recipes recommend pretreating vegetables. Unlike fruit, vegetables are pretreated primarily to tenderize them and ease drying by reducing overall dehydrating time. Pretreating vegetables does not significantly extend their shelf life.

BLANCHING   Blanch vegetables in simmering water until they are bright in color and tender-crisp (depending on the vegetable, this can be as little as 30 seconds or as much as 5 minutes). Shock the vegetables in ice water to maintain their color and stop the cooking. Drain and transfer to drying trays.

STEAMING   Place prepared vegetables in a steamer tray, cover, and steam until the vegetables are heated through (but do not steam so long that the process cooks them). Transfer the steamed vegetables to drying trays.

REHYDRATING   Dried fruits are known for their chewy texture,

VEGGIE CHIPS

Making vegetable chips is a simple, delicious way to enjoy dehydrated vegetables. Blanch or steam the vegetables, and then season them with spices or herbs. Chips can be made in the oven or dehydrator. They are crisp and tasty—so tasty that you'll have no problem eating them within the recommended 1-week storage time.

but to effectively preserve vegetables by drying, nearly all moisture is removed. Vegetables can be rehydrated in warm water, broth, wine, or another flavorful liquid. Use just enough warm liquid to cover the vegetables, rehydrate for 5 to 10 minutes, then use as directed in the recipes. Generally, all vegetables should be rehydrated if they are being used as a component of a dish, unless they are being consumed raw. Even if the dried vegetables are being added to soup, they should be properly rehydrated, or else they may be tough and unpleasant. The rehydrating liquid is often incorporated into the finished dish, because some flavor and nutrients leach into the liquid during soaking.

STORING DRIED VEGETABLES   Dried vegetables have a very short shelf life, making drying an ineffective long-term preservation method. Store in an airtight container in a cool, dry, dark place. If they show any visible signs of mold, discoloration, or shriveling, discard them. Properly stored, dried vegetables will last for 1 to 2 weeks.

HERBS AND SPICES

Herbs and spices are easy and relatively quick to dry. Wash and thoroughly dry herbs before drying. Most herbs dry well, but herbs that are very delicate or tender, such as mint, basil, or tarragon, need to be dried quickly (at a higher temperature) or they will turn brown and/or begin to spoil. Herbs can be dried in a dehydrator or in a warm room (on drying screens or tied into bunches and hung in vented paper bags). Herbs and spices recommended for drying are:

Anise	Cumin	Oregano
Basil	Dill	Parsley
Caraway Seed	Fennel	Rosemary
Celery Seed	Ginger	Sage
Chervil	Marjoram	Savory
Chives	Mint	Tarragon
Coriander/Cilantro	Mustard Seed	Thyme

STORING DRIED HERBS AND SPICES

Store dried herbs in an airtight container in a cool, dry, dark place. It is best to keep leaves and seeds whole until just before using—they will be more potent and keep longer this way. Properly stored, whole dried herbs and spices will keep for up to 1 year. Once they are ground, they will keep for only up to 6 months.

DRYING NUTS AND SEEDS

Nuts (like almonds, walnuts, and pecans) and seeds (like pumpkin and sunflower) can be dried in a dehydrator or in a warm room. They can be dried in or out of their shells. Store dried nuts and seeds in a cool, dry, dark place. They are prone to rancidity, which may be detectable only by tasting them. Properly stored, they will keep for up to 4 months. Freezing will increase their shelf life to up to 1 year.

MEAT AND FISH

Meat and fish both dry well and are commonly used to make jerky. Meat and fish should be cleaned and trimmed well before drying. Cut them into uniform strips (between ¼ and ½ inch), and season as desired (they can be seasoned using spices, herbs, brines (see page 129), or **dry cures** (see page 132). There are more safety concerns when drying meat and fish than with other foods, so it is recommended that most be heated in a preheated 175° to 185°F oven before the drying process begins to eliminate any present bacteria before exposing the meat to lower drying temperatures. Alternatively, the meat or fish can be heated in a hotter oven (250° to 275°F) after the drying process is complete. Drying temperatures for meat should be relatively high (between 140° and 160°F) to keep the process moving quickly—meat and fish need to be dried fast, before they begin to spoil. Meat and fish recommended for drying are:

* **BEEF**: Lean cuts such as flank steak, round, and sirloin dry well.
* **CURED PORK**: Drying fresh pork is not recommended, due to dangers of the presence of trichinosis, but cured pork products like ham or bacon can be dried.
* **FISH**: Most fish dries well, but take care to clean the fish properly.
* **GAME**: Elk, deer, rabbit, and other game dry well, but make sure to take extra precaution, since it easier for these meats to be contaminated.
* **LAMB**: Lean cuts like the leg or shoulder work best.

STORING DRIED MEAT AND FISH

Store dried meat and fish products in an airtight container, preferably

---

DRY CURE: Preserving an item by packing it with a mixture of salt, sweetener, flavoring, and a curing blend.

in a dry environment (be especially vigilant about spoilage if storing them in a humid environment). Properly stored, dried meat and fish products can be kept for 2 to 3 weeks at room temperature, or for up to 2 months frozen.

DRYING TECHNIQUES

There are multiple techniques for drying and dehydrating foods. Some require special equipment, while others require more time and patience.

SUN DRYING

Sun drying is an easy and natural way to dry certain foods. Very little equipment is needed— just plenty of sunshine and some time. Sun drying will take longer than using a dehydrator or oven, and it is important to be aware of elemental factors, such as pests or insects. Also be aware that without the constant, forced-air circulation of a fan (such as those used in room drying or in a dehydrator), foods drying in the sun can spoil if they are not properly tended.

Keep food in direct sunlight for the first few days—once food is partially dried, it can be in partial shade (alternatively, foods can be finished in a warm room—see the sidebar on page 101). Bring the food in at night, and return it to the sun first thing in the morning. Depending on the moisture content and size, food may take anywhere from 1 to 5 days to dry.

EQUIPMENT Basic drying trays made of food-safe materials (see sidebar, page 102) are multipurpose and can be used in sun drying. It's best to set the trays up on racks to encourage natural air circulation. Cover the racks with cheesecloth, and place the fruit evenly in a single layer on the trays. Cover the food with another layer of cheesecloth to discourage contamination from dust or pests. Foods recommended for sun drying are:

Apples	Dates	Peas
Apricots	Figs	Peas
Cherries	Grapes	Plums
Chile Peppers	Lentils	Shell Beans
Citrus Peels	Nectarines	Soybeans
Coconut	Peaches	
Currants	Pears	

Food can be dried completely in a warm room — just be sure there is proper air circulation in the room and that the food is protected from contamination.

OVEN DRYING

Oven drying can produce an array of products, from partially dried and chewy foods to completely dehydrated, crisp foods. Some foods do not respond well to oven drying. Fruits with thick skins have trouble evaporating moisture quickly enough—their skins act like a barrier. Also, foods with extremely high moisture content will never get fully dry. Recommended temperatures for most oven-drying recipes are between 100° and 130°F, though some recipes may suggest higher temperatures during early stages of drying.

DRYING COOKED MEATS

This technique was originally used to decrease the space required to store cooked meat—and dried meat is lightweight, making it ideal for campers and hikers. Choose lean cuts of meat, cook as desired, cool to room temperature, and then refrigerate for at least 1 hour. Cut the chilled meat into cubes and transfer to drying racks. Dry at a high temperature (between 140° and 160°F) until the meat is completely dried, 4 to 5 hours. Dried meat can be rehydrated in soups, stews, or casseroles.

EQUIPMENT A good oven thermometer in excellent working order is essential for oven drying. Don't trust the knob on your oven—it is not exact. Check the oven's temperature regularly, especially if it is gas (which will cause the temperature to fluctuate more rapidly). A standard drying tray works beautifully; just make sure it's made of materials that will handle the oven's more intense heat (screen, wood, and stainless steel are all excellent choices; see Resources, page 172). You may also use your oven racks (or buy extra oven racks)—just wrap them tightly with screen and/or cheesecloth. Leave 2 to 4 inches between each tray to encourage air circulation. Convection ovens are excellent, because they circulate air throughout the oven, but they are not absolutely necessary. For non-convection ovens, prop the oven door open 2 to 3 inches to allow air to circulate and moisture to escape from the oven.

DRYING WITH A DEHYDRATOR

For larger quantities, you may want to consider investing in a dehydrator, which will make quick work of any recipe. Dehydrators are fast and efficient, and most models are relatively inexpensive. They also take certain elemental factors that can be a concern with other techniques out of the equation, like bad weather, humidity, and pests. Look for a dehydrator with excellent air circulation, decent capacity, and a versatile thermostat (you want the ability to go anywhere between 80° and 160°F) that is easily adjusted.

MAKING YOUR OWN DRYING RACKS

Commercially made drying racks (such as those found in dehydrators) are perfect for any type of drying. You can buy extra racks for these purposes or source them from old, broken, or used dehydrators. However, many people elect to build their own drying racks, which is simple and inexpensive.

Use wood slats for stability, and then cover with food-safe plastic or stainless-steel screening. The mesh of this screen should be very fine, so that small foods cannot fall through. Other common screening materials (copper and aluminum, for example) should not be used, because they promote oxidization and can otherwise discolor and contaminate the food.

Each dehydrator will have different requirements and instructions for use, so read your manual carefully before attempting any of the recipes in this chapter. Remember that temperature is key with dehydrators, since they have the ability to work faster and more efficiently than other drying methods. Here's a basic guideline:

High Temps. (120° to 160°F)	Lower Temps (80° 120°F)
Meat	Nuts
Fish	Herbs
Early drying stages of fruits and vegetables	Later drying stages of fruits and vegetables

HOW TO DRY AND DEHYDRATE SAFELY

There are several safety concerns to be aware of when drying and dehydrating:

* **CONTAMINATION**: Be careful to protect food from pests, dusts, animals, chemicals, and other foods that may lead to cross contamination. This is especially important when sun drying or room drying, where the food is more exposed to such elements.

* **TEMPERATURE DANGER ZONE**: Most drying recipes keep food between 80° and 160°F for an extended period, which keeps food right in the middle of the temperature danger zone. If food stays in this zone for longer than 4 hours, the chances of it becoming contaminated by bacteria are extremely high. Monitor food closely and follow safety instructions. Large food items that may take longer to dry should be cut into smaller pieces so that they

DRYING IN A WARM ROOM

A technique often used for drying flowers, drying in a warm room can also be used for drying various foods, especially herbs and nuts. Other, partially dried foods can be finished in a warm room. Only use this technique in an environment low in humidity, and keep the temperature around 80°F during the entire drying process. Keep a fan near the food for constant, even air circulation. Place food on drying trays (see page 102) or hung in ventilated paper bags (see page 97). Like sun drying, this technique can take some time—depending on the food being dried, up to 3 days.

can dehydrate more rapidly. Products like meat and fish can be heated in an oven before the dehydrating process begins to shorten drying time and prevent the growth of bacteria or other pathogens. Focus on proper air circulation, which will reduce drying time as well as the chances for contamination.

* **SPOILAGE:** Many dried foods do not have a long shelf life. Follow storage instructions carefully and keep an eye out for signs of spoilage or rancidity.

DRIED HERBS

It is best to cut herbs the day you plan on drying them. You can place the tied bunches into a paper bag before hanging them—this protects them from moisture and light. But be sure to cut vents in the bag to promote air circulation.

MAKES 1 BUNCH

1 bunch herbs

1 Cut the herbs long enough to be dried suspended, 5 to 8 inches.
2 Rinse the herbs gently under cold water, and shake off excess water. Tie the herbs by the stem into small bunches and hang them upside down in a warm, dry, dark place. Be sure the space allows for good air circulation—you can create this yourself with a fan, if needed (see page 101).
3 Hang the herbs until they are thoroughly dry. The total time will depend on the herb and the size of the bunches. When the herbs are dry, you can remove leaves from their stems and store in airtight containers.

STORAGE:
The dried herbs will keep, stored in airtight containers, for up to 6 months.

DRIED KALE CHIPS

A tasty, healthy, and wonderfully crisp alternative to potato chips.

MAKES ABOUT 4 OZ

1 bunch kale, coarsely chopped

2 tbsp olive oil

Kosher salt and freshly ground black pepper, as needed

1   Preheat the oven to 325°F. Line a baking sheet with parchment paper.

2   In a large bowl, toss the kale with the olive oil to coat. Season with salt and pepper.

3   Transfer the kale to the prepared baking sheet, being sure to place the pieces in a single layer without crowding or overlapping.

4   Bake until the kale has browned slightly and is very crisp, about 15 minutes. Let cool before serving.

VARIATIONS:

OVEN-DRIED CHARD CHIPS: Replace the kale with 1 bunch of coarsely chopped Swiss chard.

OVEN-DRIED SPINACH CHIPS: Replace the kale with 2 bunches of stemmed spinach leaves.

STORAGE:

These chips will keep for up to 2 weeks if kept dry in an airtight container.

DRIED POTATO CHIPS

Try adding herbs or spices for more flavorful chips.

MAKES ABOUT 4 OZ

¼ cup olive oil

1½ lb potatoes

Kosher salt and freshly ground black pepper, as needed

1   Preheat the oven to 400°F. Coat a baking sheet with half of the olive oil.

2   Slice the potatoes very thin (about ⅛ inch thick), using a mandoline. Transfer to a large bowl, and toss with the remaining olive oil. Season with salt and pepper.

3   Transfer the potatoes to the prepared baking sheet, being careful to place in a single layer without overlapping or overcrowding.

4   Bake until the chips are golden brown and crisp, 20 to 25 minutes. Let cool before serving.

VARIATIONS:

OVEN-DRIED SWEET POTATO CHIPS: Replace the potatoes with sweet potatoes.
OVEN-DRIED PARSNIPS: Replace the potatoes with parsnips.

STORAGE:

These chips will keep for up to 2 weeks if kept dry in an airtight container.

DRIED CHILES

Instead of seeding the peppers and oven-drying or sun-drying them, use a large needle to string the whole chiles onto heavy thread by their stems. The strung chiles can be hung and dried in a warm, dry, dark room.

MAKES ABOUT 4 OZ

1 lb fresh chile peppers, seeded
    and halved

1   Chiles can be dried in a dehydrator, in the oven, or in the sun. Place the halved chiles onto drying racks or screens and dry as directed in your chosen technique (see page 99).

2   Dry the chiles between 90° and 100°F. The total time will depend on the size of the chiles. As they dry, their skins will shrivel and become dark. Store finished dried chiles in an airtight container.

STORAGE:

These chiles will keep for up to 3 weeks if kept dry in an airtight container. You may freeze them for up to 2 months, but their texture may be slightly altered when thawed.

DRIED MUSHROOMS

Dried mushrooms can be reconstituted in warm water or broth. Since the liquid used to rehydrate them becomes very flavorful, try to incorporate it into your finished dish.

MAKES ABOUT 5 OZ

3 lb mushrooms, cleaned and
    trimmed

1 Mushrooms can be dried in a dehydrator, in the oven, or in the sun. Place the mushrooms onto drying racks or screens and dry as directed in your chosen technique (see page 99).

2 Start drying between 85° and 95°F. When the mushrooms are partially dried (slightly leathery on the outer surface), raise the temperature to 125°F. The total drying time will depend on the size of the mushrooms. Store finished dried mushrooms in an airtight container.

STORAGE:

These mushrooms keep for up to 3 weeks if kept dry in an airtight container. You may freeze them for up to 2 months, but their texture may be slightly altered when thawed.

DRIED GARLIC

Garlic is generally harvested between July and August, and most commercially sold heads of garlic are already dried. If you grow your own garlic and want to extend its shelf life, use this simple technique. Hard/stiff-neck varieties must be used and/or consumed within 1 month of harvest. Soft-neck varieties can be dried, braided (if desired), and stored for longer periods of time.

MAKES 3 LB

3 lb freshly harvested garlic
     bulbs

1   Spread the bulbs out in an even layer in a cool, dry, dark place with moderate ventilation.
2   Allow to dry for 7 to 10 days, or until the outer skin is completely dry.

STORAGE:
Dried garlic will keep in a cool, dry, dark place for up to 8 months.

OVEN-DRIED TOMATOES

You can make oil-packed tomatoes by tightly packing dried tomatoes in a storage container and adding enough extra-virgin olive oil to cover.

MAKES ABOUT 8 OZ

2 lb tomatoes, halved or
    quartered

1   Pretreat the tomatoes, if desired (see page 98). Preheat the oven to 140°F. Transfer the tomatoes to oven drying racks or baking sheets lined with aluminum foil.

2   Place the tomatoes in the oven, and prop the door open about 4 inches. Allow the tomatoes to cook until completely dried. The total drying time will depend on the size of the tomatoes. Store finished dried tomatoes in airtight containers.

VARIATION:

SUN-DRIED TOMATOES: Place the tomatoes on drying racks and follow the directions for sun drying on page 99.

STORAGE:

These tomatoes will keep for up to 3 weeks if kept dry. You may freeze them for up to 2 months, but their texture may be slightly altered when thawed. Oil-packed dried tomatoes will keep, refrigerated, for up to 1 month.

FRUIT LEATHER

You can use almost any kind of fruit for this recipe; just peel, core, and/or remove seeds as necessary. Try combining different fruit purees, adding a small amount of sweetener, or mixing in some spices or extracts to create new and interesting flavors.

MAKES ABOUT 4 OZ

5 cups pureed fruit   4 tbsp fresh lemon juice

1   Depending on the type of fruit you are using, you may want to strain the pureed fruit mixture to remove pulp, tiny seeds, and so forth.

2   In a large bowl, stir the lemon juice into the fruit puree. If you are using additional flavoring ingredients, stir them in at this time.

3   Line two baking sheets with silicone mats. Divide the fruit mixture between the two baking sheets and spread into a thin, even layer (about ¼ inch thick).

4   Dry the fruit in a dehydrator or oven at 135°F until dry, 2 to 3 hours. The finished leather should be dry but still chewy. Let cool, then transfer to airtight storage containers.

STORAGE:

Fruit leather will keep, wrapped in waxed paper and stored in an airtight container, for up to 1 month. It will also keep frozen for up to 6 months.

BEEF JERKY WITH ANISE AND CHILE

This jerky combines a variety of flavors for a unique finished product.

MAKES ABOUT 1½ LB

1½ cups brewed oolong tea

1½ cups cola

¼ cup maple syrup

2 tbsp anise seed, crushed

2 tbsp red pepper flakes

1 cup soy sauce

½ cup Worcestershire sauce

½ cup fresh lime juice

¼ cup fish sauce

2 lb beef top round

1   In a large pot, bring the tea, cola, syrup, anise, and red pepper flakes to a simmer over medium-low heat. Simmer until the mixture has reduced by half.

2   Transfer the mixture to a large, shallow dish and let cool to room temperature.

3   Stir in the soy sauce, Worcestershire, lime juice, and fish sauce.

4   Cut the meat across the grain into thin slices, about ¼ inch thick. The strips should be about 8 inches long and 2 inches wide. Add the strips to the marinade, and toss to coat. Cover with plastic wrap and refrigerate for 6 to 8 hours.

5   Preheat the oven to 200°F. Remove the beef from the marinade and pat dry with paper towels.

6   Transfer the beef to a wire rack set on a baking sheet. Dry in the oven until the jerky is firm and dry but still chewy, 2 to 3 hours. Let cool completely before storing in an airtight container.

STORAGE:

This jerky will keep at room temperature for up to 2 weeks if kept dry. You may freeze it for up to 2 months, but the texture may be slightly altered when thawed.

BEEF JERKY

Buffalo, venison, or other red game meat can be used instead of the beef. Most lean cuts, such as leg cuts, are appropriate.

MAKES ABOUT 1 LB

3 lb top round beef

1 cup brewed coffee

1 cup Worcestershire sauce

1 cup ketchup

½ cup apple cider vinegar

5 oz honey

½ cup light brown sugar

2 tbsp chili powder

3 tsp kosher salt

2 tsp sweet paprika

2 tsp onion powder

2 tsp red pepper flakes

1 tsp freshly ground
    black pepper

1 tsp garlic powder

1   Cut the beef across the grain into thin strips, about ¼ inch thick. The strips should be about 8 inches long and 2 inches wide.

2   In a medium bowl, combine the remaining ingredients. Pour the marinade into a sealable plastic bag, and add the meat. Marinate the meat, refrigerated, for 24 hours.

3   Preheat the oven to 200°F. Transfer the beef to a wire rack set on a baking sheet. Pat the meat dry.

4   Dry in the oven for 1 hour. Turn the jerky over, and continue to cook until completely dry, 1 to 1½ hours more.

5   Let cool completely before storing in an airtight container.

NOTE:

The meat may be frozen prior to cutting to make thin slicing easier. The meat can also be placed in marinade and frozen. Thaw the frozen meat in the refrigerator overnight before cooking.

STORAGE:

This jerky will keep for up to 2 weeks if kept dry. You may freeze it for up to 2 months, but the texture may be slightly altered when thawed.

CARNE SECA

Carne seca, or "dried meat," is a flavorful jerky—feel free to add more spice to taste.

MAKES ABOUT 8 OZ

1 lb beef top round,
    sliced ⅛ thick

¼ cup fresh lime juice

¼ cup soy sauce

1 tbsp kosher salt

1 tbsp chili powder

2 tsp onion powder

2 tsp garlic powder

1   Pound the sliced meat lightly with a tenderizer or mallet. Transfer the meat to a shallow container.

2   In a medium bowl, combine the lime juice, soy sauce, salt, chili powder, onion powder, and garlic powder.

3   Pour this mixture over the meat and mix well to combine. Let the meat marinate, refrigerated, for 30 minutes.

4   Preheat the oven to 175°F. Transfer the meat to a baking sheet and cook in the oven until the meat is dry, 1½ to 2 hours. Let cool completely, then store in an airtight container.

STORAGE:

This jerky will keep for up to 2 weeks if kept dry. You may freeze it for up to 2 months, but the texture may be slightly altered when thawed.

TURKEY JERKY

The meat can be frozen prior to cutting to make thin slicing easier.

MAKES ABOUT 1 LB

2 lb boneless, skinless
    turkey breast

1 cup chicken broth

½ cup soy sauce

2 tbsp Worcestershire sauce

¼ cup packed light brown sugar

1 tbsp freshly ground
    black pepper

2 tsp garlic powder

1 tsp cayenne pepper

1 Place the turkey between sheets of waxed paper and pound it thin with a meat tenderizer. Cut the tenderized turkey across the grain into thin strips, about ¼ inch thick. The strips should be about 8 inches long and 2 inches wide.

2 In a medium bowl, combine the remaining ingredients. Pour the marinade into a sealable plastic bag, and add the turkey. Marinate the meat in the refrigerator for 24 hours.

3 Preheat the oven to 200°F. Transfer the turkey to a wire rack set on a baking sheet.

4 Dry in the oven for 1 hour. Turn the jerky over, and continue to cook until completely dry, 1 to 1½ hours more.

5 Let cool completely before storing in an airtight container.

NOTE:

The meat can be placed in the marinade and then frozen. Thaw the frozen meat in the refrigerator overnight before cooking.

STORAGE:

This jerky will keep for up to 2 weeks if kept dry. You may freeze it for up to 2 months, but the texture may be slightly altered when thawed.

DRIED APRICOTS

Dried fruit is easy to make and makes a tasty snack anytime! This method will work for most fruits (see recommended varieties for drying on page 93).

MAKES ABOUT 1 LB

3 lb apricots, halved and pitted

1 Pretreat the fruit as desired (see page 94). Transfer the fruit to drying racks.

2 Dry in a dehydrator set at 130°F until the apricots are dry and chewy. The total drying time will depend on the size of the apricots. Store finished dried apricots in airtight containers.

VARIATIONS:

DRIED CHERRIES: Replace the apricots with cherries.

RAISINS: Replace the apricots with grapes.

DRIED PEARS: Replace the apricots with pears.

DRIED MANGOS: Replace the apricots with mangos.

STORAGE:

The fruit will keep for up to 2 weeks if kept dry. You may freeze it for up to 1 month, but the texture may be slightly altered when thawed.

BRINING, CURING, AND SMOKING

This chapter discusses techniques that not only preserve foods, but also impart an array of unique flavors that create delicious results.

SMOKING   Smoking provides a delicious flavor to a variety of foods: meat, fish, cheeses, and more. Many factors affect the flavor — the technique, the type of wood used, and the length of the smoking time — and smoking at home gives you the opportunity to experiment with these factors to create a tasty end result.

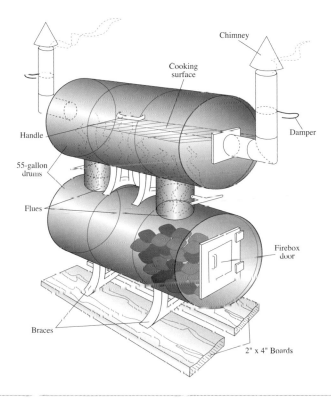

This large smoker shows all the components that are ideal for properly smoking food.

CREATING THE SMOKE

Smoky fires are created by controlling oxygen: A decrease in oxygen causes wood to smolder and smoke. An overexposure to oxygen will cause the temperature inside the smoker to rise without much smoke, which will cook the food faster and will result in a less smoky flavor. The addition of moisture through the use of damp products (such as heavily soaked wood chips) will cause smoldering rather than burning, which creates more smoke.

EQUIPMENT

There are many varieties of smokers available, so consider the following factors when purchasing or building your smoker:

* How much do you plan on smoking and how frequently do you plan to use your smoker? This will help determine the type and size of smoker you should choose.
* What is your budget? Smokers are available in a variety of price ranges, but sometimes a lower price means a smaller unit.
* What type of fuel do you intend to use? Some smokers use wood, others use charcoal or propane, and some even use electricity.
* Where are you going to store your unit? This may determine the size and model best suited to your space.

SMOKERS   Smokers may be purchased in many home improvement, outdoor supply, and gourmet kitchen supply stores (see Resources, page 172). They are also called smoke ovens or smokehouses. While they come in a variety of shapes and sizes, the basic setup is the same: There is a central chamber for the food and a heat source (usually at the bottom), an element to control the amount of air that enters the smoke chamber, and a temperature gauge. Smokers can be heated using multiple sources, such as electricity, propane, charcoal, and wood. They come in an array of sizes and materials, all of which can work wonderfully depending on the amount and frequency of your smoking.

ADJUSTING SMOKERS FOR COLD SMOKING

Most smokers are created for hot smoking, and thus, adjustments need to be made in order to use them for **cold smoking**. If you plan on cold smoking frequently, you may want to construct your own permanent cold-smoking unit (see Resources, page 172). When cold smoking, the heat source should not be connected directly under the chamber or products will begin to cook as they smoke. A pipe or tunnel should be added to funnel smoke into the smoker while controlling the overall temperature of the smoker.

COLD SMOKING: A method in which food is flavored with smoke without cooking the item.

DUAL-CHAMBER SMOKERS OR BARBECUE

GRILLS   Dual-chamber smokers and some barbecue grills can also act as smokers—they either have an additional chamber for smoking or they simply allow for proper temperature control within the main vessel of the grill. These units are excellent simply for their versatility – they can be used not only for smoking, but also for grilling, barbecuing, and slow cooking (see Resources, page 172).

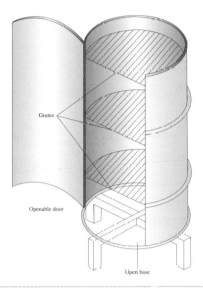

Grates

Openable door

Open base

This smaller, homemade model also has all of the primary components needed to smoke food.

OTHER SMOKE-PRODUCING ITEMS

Though the woods listed on page 125 are the most common items used to smoke foods, there are other products that produce excellent and flavorful smoke. Grapevines are excellent for smoking and produce flavors similar to those of other fruitwoods like apple or cherry. Wine barrel chips impart not only oaky flavors from the wood, but also deeply aromatic smoke due to the contact with wine. Dried seaweed makes an excellent smoke that is wonderful with fish and seafood. Herbs, spices, and other aromatics can also be used to create a very aromatic smoke that is ideal for smaller pieces or amounts of food.

HOMEMADE SMOKERS Homemade smokers can be simple or complex to construct. Popular homemade versions are:

* **Smokehouses:** Resembling a small shed, this unit allows a large space for smoking.
* **Outdoor Ovens:** Building an outdoor oven with a chimney can result in an excellent smoker.
* **Steel Drum Smokers:** A clean steel drum with a door cut into it to place a heating unit is a simple solution for homemade smoking.
* **Converted Refrigerator Smokers:** An old refrigerator can make an ideal smoking environment. Remove the motors in both the freezer and refrigerator compartments. Remove the insulation if you plan on using the unit primarily for hot smoking (if you plan on using it for cold smoking, you can leave the insulation in). For hot smoking, line the refrigerator with bricks to hold in heat. Remove the base of the refrigerator and place it over a fire pit. You may also want to cut a hole somewhere in the refrigerator to provide a source of oxygen to control heat and smoke levels.

WOODS FOR SMOKING Hardwoods are ideal for smoking—they produce a good, constant smoke and provide excellent flavor and aroma. Soft or resinous woods should not be used, as they can flare up, burn without producing smoke, alter the color of the food, or produce bitter and unpleasant flavors. Each wood imparts a

PROPERTIES OF SMOKE

Smoke is a complex production of compounds and has various effects on food. Contact with the smoke preserves food by applying **antimicrobial compounds** to its surface, which prevents the growth of mold or bacteria. Some of these compounds also prevent oxidation, which extends the overall shelf life and quality of the food. Smoke also alters the color of food due to the combined effects of heating, drying, and the application of various compounds as the food smokes. And perhaps most importantly, smoke provides a unique aroma and flavor to foods. Be aware, however, that excessive smoke can create an unpleasant, bitter flavor in most foods.

ANTIMICROBIAL COMPOUNDS: Compounds introduced by smoke that cling to the outside of foods, which protects the surface by preventing the growth of mold or bacteria.

unique and distinct flavor to the food being smoked. Wood for smoking is commonly available in four forms: chips, nuggets, chunks, and sawdust. Be sure to purchase wood that is meant for smoking, as some woods have been treated with chemicals or may be otherwise contaminated and should not be used with food. Some woods that are ideal for smoking are:

Alder	Mesquite
Apple	Peach
Cherry	Pear
Hickory	Pecan
Maple	

TECHNIQUES

COLD SMOKING

Cold smoking is a method in which food is flavored with smoke without cooking the item. Cold smoking is usually done between 70° and 100°F, but this temperature puts food in the danger zone. Therefore, food cannot be cold smoked at this temperature for longer than 2 hours without potentially exposing it to contamination. Because of this, the ideal temperature is around 40°F, because it allows products to cold smoke for longer periods of time. It is often recommended that items that are to be cold smoked should be cured because **curing** reduces the possibility of contamination and food-borne illnesses such as botulism.

HOT SMOKING

The method of hot smoking flavors food with smoke and also cooks the items. This method is much simpler than cold smoking, because the internal temperature of the smoking vessel does not need to be monitored quite as closely as when an item is cold smoked.

GENERAL SMOKING TECHNIQUES

Prepare items to be smoked as dictated by the recipe (this may involve trimming excess fat, trussing or tying, boning large cuts of meat, or generally cleaning the item). If desired, cure or brine the

---

CURING: A drying process in which moisture is removed from food (generally meat) through the application of a dry cure.

item to be smoked. Rinse the item, and dry it well (a wet surface will not absorb smoke). Once the item is completely prepared, proceed with the specific instructions to smoke the item. Remember that the type of item will dictate how it should be smoked (larger items may need to be hung or placed on racks to smoke) and for how long.

MAKING SAUSAGES

One of the tastiest items to make and smoke at home is sausage. Following are detailed instructions for foolproof homemade sausage.

EQUIPMENT

Sausages were once made entirely by hand, but modern sausage making involves a variety of tools and equipment. The primary equipment necessary includes:

MEAT GRINDER Grinders can be sold as attachments to other common household appliances (such as mixers and food processors). The main thing to look for when purchasing a grinder is the ability to grind at multiple thicknesses to ensure ease of preparation. Most come with three plates: coarse—⅜ inch, medium—¼ inch, and fine—⅛ inch, (see Resources, page 172).

SAUSAGE STUFFER This tool is usually hand-cranked and is used to easily funnel product into casings (see Resources, page 172).

FOOD PROCESSOR It is ideal for making emulsified sausages but also is useful in other methods.

STAND MIXER Most sausage recipes in this chapter require mixing in a stand mixer after grinding. Make sure yours has the capacity to hold the amount of product you're working with, or you may need to work in batches.

TEASING NEEDLE/PRICKER This small tool is made up of a long, thin needle attached to a handle. It's used to poke small holes in sausage casings to remove excess air and/or to remove air pockets from sausages after stuffing (see Resources, page 172).

CASINGS

Casings can be natural (derived from animals—usually sheep, pigs, or cows) or artificial (plastic, paper, and so on). They can be edible or nonedible, depending on the materials used to make them. In this book, we recommend using natural animal casings. These types of casings are sold in bundles called "hanks," either by the type of animal they come from or by their stuffing capacity.

To prepare the casings for use, follow these instructions:

1. If the casings have been sold in hanks, you must carefully unwind the hank to be sure it is free of tangles. When you've successfully untangled a length of casing, wrap it around four fingers to create a bundle. These bundles can be stored in salt, in the refrigerator, until needed (they will keep for up to 1 year). Casings not sold in hanks can also be handled and stored in this fashion.

2. When ready to use the casings, weigh the product to be stuffed to determine the amount of casings you will need. Reconstitute the casings in warm water (thicker-walled casings will need more reconstituting time than thin-walled casings), and gently place one end of the casing on the sausage stuffer.

3. Fill the casing with the sausage mixture. Pinch and tie the end of the casing to enclose the sausage inside. At this point, you can measure lengths to create links in the sausage. Create the links by pinching the sausage where you want a link to form, and gently twist the casing several times to secure. Remember that the larger a casing is, the thicker the walls of the sausage will be, and when you dry or smoke the sausage, the casing will dry out and become harder and/or brittle. Choose the type of casing that is best for the desired result of the sausage you are making (see Resources, page 172).

BASIC GRINDING, MIXING, AND STUFFING

1. Sanitize and chill the equipment. This will prevent the growth of bacteria and will also ease the grinding process.

2. Prepare the meat and fat to be ground. Be sure they are properly chilled and diced to the recommended size.

3. Prepare the seasonings or other ingredients. Toss the seasonings with the meat; this will ensure they are evenly distributed as the meat is ground.

4. Refrigerate or briefly freeze the meat. This makes the meat easier to grind and also prevents the growth of bacteria.

5. Assemble the grinder.

6. Grind the meat into a chilled container (or a bowl set over an ice bath). Do not force the meat through the grinder—it should grind easily through the plate(s) designated by the recipe.

7. Add ice or cold liquid as directed by the recipe. This replenishes moisture and helps to distribute seasonings throughout the meat.

8. Mix the sausage mixture as directed by the recipe. The finished sausage mixture should be sticky.

9. Cook a sample to test the seasoning. This is optional, but it can be useful especially when making large batches.

10. Stuff the sausage mixture into reconstituted casings (see page 127), form into patties, or otherwise mold into the desired shape.

STORING GUIDELINES AND SUGGESTIONS FOR SMOKED FOODS

While the process of smoking is seen as a preserving technique, smoked foods do not automatically have a longer shelf life than raw foods. Smoked meats and fish should be kept in the refrigerator for short-term storage or in the freezer for long-term storage. Smoked poultry and meat will keep for up to 2 weeks in the refrigerator or 6 to 12 months in the freezer. Smoked fish will keep for up to 1 week in the refrigerator or for up to 3 months in the freezer. Wrap foods tightly with a layer of plastic wrap, then with a layer of aluminum foil. See specific recipes for more detailed storage guidelines.

BRINING: A means of preserving in which a food is either submerged in or injected with a wet cure.

CURING AND BRINING

Curing and **brining** are two techniques that add an incredible amount of flavor to foods. Curing is essentially a drying process in which moisture is removed from food (generally meat) through the application of a dry cure. The process takes a bit of time, but it extends the shelf life of food due to the lack of moisture in the finished product. Brining is also a curing method, and it is often referred to as "wet curing." Traditionally, brines were simply a mixture of water and salt. Modern brines, however, include additional flavoring ingredients (sweeteners, juices, vinegars, herbs, spices, and so on can be added to a brine) to produce a more flavorful end result.

INGREDIENTS

WATER   Brines should be made with filtered or distilled water. Other liquids, including beer, wine, vinegar, or juices can replace part of the water in a brine depending on the recipe.

SALT   Salt is hygroscopic, which means it is capable of drawing moisture out of foods. That is why it is the primary ingredient in dry cures and brines. Salt should not be iodized and should not have additives such as anti-caking agents. For this reason, the most recommended salt is kosher salt. Kosher salt has no additives, and it also has larger crystals than some other salts, which makes it ideal for absorbing moisture and curing foods.

Spread one third of the cure in the base of a container large enough to fit the product to be cured. Place the food on top, then cover with the remaining cure.

THE PELLICLE

Pellicle is a term used to identify the dried skin on the flesh of fish or meat that has been cured. After the curing and rinsing, food should be given substantial time to dry in a cool place. The pellicle forms during this time. It serves multiple purposes:

* It forms a "seal" around the food, which keeps natural fats inside the flesh. When these fats rise to the surface, they can promote spoilage.
* The same "seal" helps retain natural moisture so that the food does not dry out during smoking.
* During smoking, the flavor of the smoke adheres to the pellicle, resulting in a more flavorful finished product.

NITRITES   Nitrites are naturally present in sodium and potassium and play three key roles in curing and brining. In the early days of curing and brining, nitrites were found in the unrefined salt commonly used in the preservation processes. The nitrites reacted with the myoglobin (a protein that forms a pigment that gives meat its color) to create the signature reddish hue found on cured foods. In addition to affecting color, nitrates also give cured and brined foods a unique flavor and prevent the development of food-borne illnesses, including botulism. Most recipes in this book call for Insta Cure No. 1 (a curing blend that contains nitrites). Another variety available is called TCM (Tinted Curing Mixture); pink salt and **curing salt** are general names for this type of product. All of these items can be found at specialty grocery stores, and nitrates can also be found in commercially sold cures, which are available in most grocery stores and through various online retailers (see Resources, page 172).

SWEETENERS   Sweeteners are not added to every dry cure or brine, but they are a popular addition for the excellent flavor they add to the finished product. In addition, sweeteners promote the curing process, balance the saltiness of the brine or dry cure, and are also hygroscopic (so they aid in drawing out moisture). Different sweeteners will yield different results, but some popular options include white sugar, brown sugar, maple sugar, honey, and molasses.

SEASONINGS   Any additional seasonings may be added to cures and brines, depending on the desired end result. Herbs (such

---

CURING SALT: A mixture of 94 percent table salt (sodium chloride) and 6 percent sodium nitrite, used to preserve meats. Also known as tinted curing mix or TCM.

as rosemary, bay leaf, or sage), spices (such as cumin, coriander, or cardamom), seeds (such as dill, mustard, or fennel), and other ingredients (such as onion, garlic, or chiles) all make excellent additions to brines and cures.

EQUIPMENT

Curing and brining are two techniques that require very little equipment. The main thing to consider is storage space, as items need to be held under refrigeration both during the process and after it is finished.

POTS   Some recipes require brines to be heated. This may be to dissolve sugar or infuse herbs or other seasonings into the brine. Be sure you have a pot large enough to accommodate your brine.

CONTAINERS FOR BRINING AND CURING   Items to be brined must be submerged in brine for the allotted amount of time. Be sure to use a container made of food-safe, noncorrosive materials that is large enough to accommodate the item being preserved as well as the brine or dry cure.

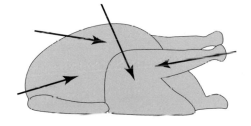

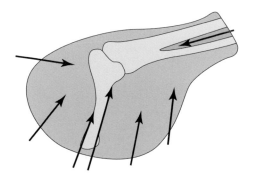

Brine should be injected into one of these areas to ensure that it thoroughly penetrates the meat.

BRINE NEEDLE   A **brine needle** is needed for use with the brine pumping method (see page 133). Most available needles are made of stainless steel so that they can be easily used and cleaned (see Resources, page 172).

TECHNIQUES

DRY CURING   Dry curing is a simple process that takes a little time and very little effort. To dry cure foods, prepare the item as necessary. Fish needs to be scored lightly with a paring knife to help the cure penetrate the flesh. Pack the cure onto the product (you will need 8 ounces of cure for every 10 pounds of the item that is being cured). Refrigerate the item, and allow it to cure for the recommended amount of time (the total time will vary depending on the size, shape, and weight of the product; see specific recipes for details). Rinse the item in lukewarm water, and allow it to air dry so that it forms a pellicle (see sidebar, page 130). The item is now ready to be used or further prepared (smoked).

Approximate Curing Times

ITEM	APPROXIMATE THICKNESS/ WEIGHT	CURE TIME
General	¼ inch thick	1–2 hours
General	½ inch thick	3–4 hours
General	1 inch thick	4–8 hours
Pork belly	1½ inches thick	7–10 days
Ham, bone-in	15–18 lb	40–45 days
Shrimp or scallops	½–1 inch	½–1 hour
Fish fillet	1–1½ lb	2 hours
Salmon fillet	2½ lb	6–12 hours
Whole fish	3–4 lb	4–6 hours

BRINE NEEDLE: A needle (usually stainless steel) used during brine pumping.

BRINE PUMPING: A method of curing in which brine is injected into the food item using a specified brine needle.

BASIC BRINING Basic brining is a simple process. Mix your brine as instructed by the recipe. If the recipe requires the brine to be heated before use, be sure to properly chill the brine before using it. Be sure the item to be brined is prepared as required by the recipe, and place it in a container that is deep enough to accommodate the item and the brine. Pour the brine over the item, and be sure it is completely submerged (some recipes may recommend that you place something on top of the item and weigh it down to ensure that it stays submerged). Keep the item submerged, in the refrigerator, for the required amount of time (the total brining time will vary depending on the thickness of the item, its density, and the amount of fat cover; see specific recipes for details).

BRINE PUMPING The brine-pumping technique has risen in popularity because it adds incredible flavor and reduces the amount of time an item needs to be brined. Use a needle specifically meant for use with **brine pumping**, and use 10 percent of the item's weight in brine solution. Insert the needle into the prepared (chilled) brine and fill the needle with brine. Inject the needle into the main item at its thickest point, inserting the needle as close to the bone (if applicable) as possible. Transfer the item to a container large enough to accommodate the item, and submerge it in brine. Hold the item submerged, in the refrigerator, for the required amount of time (the total brining time will vary; see specific recipes for details).

Brine pump with needle properly stored

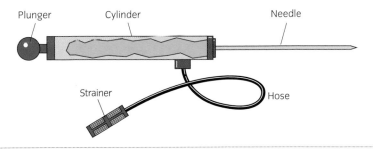

A standard brine pump

BASIC BRINING: A method of curing in which an item is completely submerged in a saltwater solution.

Approximate Brining Times for Meat

ITEM	BASIC BRINE	BRINE PUMPING
Chicken or duck pieces	1–2 hours	n/a
Whole chicken or duck	24–36 hours	12–16 hours
Pork	5–6 days	2–3 days
Whole turkey	5–6 days	3 days
Boneless ham	6 days	4 days
Bone-in ham	20–24 days	6–7 days

STORING GUIDELINES AND SUGGESTIONS FOR BRINED AND CURED FOODS

Brined and cured products have a longer shelf life, but they should still be stored in the refrigerator (under 40°F) or they will spoil. Most items should be wrapped tightly and/or stored in airtight containers and reserved in the refrigerator until ready to serve.

HOW TO SMOKE, BRINE, AND CURE SAFELY

CROSS CONTAMINATION

Since you will most likely be using your smoker for a variety of foods, be sure to clean your smoker and all tools properly to prevent **cross contamination** of future smoking projects.

TEMPERATURE DANGER ZONE

Foods that are brined, cured, or smoked can be highly susceptible to the **temperature danger zone**. Be sure to keep foods at the proper temperatures before, during, and after preparation in any of these methods. This concern is especially prominent for cold smoking, where foods can be held in the danger zone for too long if the temperature is not closely monitored.

FOOD-BORNE ILLNESSES

Food-borne illnesses can be a concern with all of the methods in this chapter, but particularly with curing. Botulism is a particular concern (especially with cold smoking). Be sure to follow proper method and storage instructions to avoid food-borne illnesses.

SPOILAGE

Brining, curing, and smoking are processes that should, if executed properly, extend a food's shelf life. However, all of these techniques take time, and spoilage may begin to occur. One of the most common signs of spoilage on these types of food is mold. If you see mold begin to appear on the outer surface of any foods, remove it by gently rubbing the food with some vinegar or white wine. If mold persists, it may be necessary to throw out the food. In addition to the length of time these processes take, there are other ways a food can become spoiled if it is not properly stored. Be sure to follow detailed storage instructions at all times.

CROSS CONTAMINATION: This occurs when a harmful substance is transferred from one surface to another. The best way to prevent cross contamination is to be as sanitary as possible throughout preparation and cooking.

TEMPERATURE DANGER ZONE: An environment between 41° and 135°F in which bacteria and other pathogens thrive.

FOOD-BORNE ILLNESSES: Caused by chemical (such as cleaning products) or physical (such as glass) contaminants that accidentally find their way into prepared foods. The most common contaminants in preserving methods are biological, which include toxins and pathogens, such as fungi, viruses, parasites, and bacteria. These are the primary causes of food-borne illnesses.

BASIC BRINE

This simple brine is ideal for most types of poultry and meat.

MAKES ABOUT 2 QUARTS

2 quarts (8 cups) water

1 cup kosher salt

1 cup light brown sugar

1 tbsp black peppercorns, smashed

2 sprigs thyme

1 sprig rosemary

2 bay leaves

1 Combine all of the ingredients in a large pot. Bring to a simmer, stirring occasionally. Simmer until the sugar and salt are completely dissolved.

2 Cool the brine completely before using.

STORAGE:

The finished brine will keep, refrigerated, for up to 1 month.

BASIC CURE

Try adding spices to this basic cure for a more flavorful end result.

MAKES ABOUT 2 CUPS

1 cup kosher salt

⅔ cup sugar

2 tbsp Insta Cure No. 1 (page 130)

In a small bowl, mix together all of the ingredients to combine. Transfer to a storage container until ready to use.

STORAGE:

The finished cure will keep in an airtight container at room temperature for up to 1 month.

APPLE CIDER BRINE

❉ ❉

This brine is excellent for use in holiday recipes.

MAKES ABOUT 2 GALLONS

1 gallon apple cider

10 cups sugar

6 cups kosher salt

5 cups water

1 bunch fresh thyme

½ cup coarsely ground black pepper

12 bay leaves

1 cinnamon stick

5 juniper berries

In a large container, combine all the ingredients. Store the brine, refrigerated, until ready to use.

VARIATION:

CRANBERRY–APPLE CIDER BRINE: Replace 3 cups of the apple cider with cranberry juice, and reduce the sugar by half.

STORAGE:

The finished brine will keep, refrigerated, for up to 1 month.

GRAVLAX

One of the most popular cured foods, this dish is simple and flavorful. Enjoy it with your favorite bagels and spreads.

MAKES 2½ LB

1 salmon fillet, skin on (about 3 lb)

8 oz kosher salt

4 oz sugar

2 tbsp freshly ground black pepper

1 tbsp onion powder

1 tsp crushed bay leaf

1 tsp ground mace

1 tsp ground cloves

½ tsp ground allspice

1   Remove the pinbones from the salmon and place it skin side down on a large piece of cheesecloth, parchment paper, or plastic wrap.

2   In a medium bowl, combine the salt, sugar, pepper, onion powder, bay leaf, mace, cloves, and allspice. Pack the cure mixture evenly over the salmon, using a thinner layer of cure as the fillet tapers at the tail.

3   Wrap the salmon loosely in the cheesecloth and place it on a baking sheet. Cure, refrigerated, for 2 days.

4   After curing, scrape off excess cure and gently rinse the salmon with cool water. Blot dry with paper towels.

5   Place the salmon on a cooling rack on a baking sheet and refrigerate overnight.

6   Cold smoke the salmon at 100°F until cooked through, about 5 hours. The salmon may be used immediately, or tightly wrapped in plastic wrap and stored.

STORAGE:
The cured salmon will keep, refrigerated, for up to 1 week.

SALT COD

A very traditional preserved food, salt cod makes a great addition to a variety of dishes.

MAKES 1½ LB

2 lb skinless cod fillets   1 cup kosher salt

1   In a large container or on a baking sheet, dredge the fish liberally with the salt. Rub the salt firmly into the fillet.

2   Wrap the fish in two layers of cheesecloth. Place the wrapped fish on a cooling or roasting rack set in a casserole dish or on a baking sheet.

3   Transfer the fish to the refrigerator and let it cure for 3 days.

4   Rinse the fish gently with cold water. Dry well and wrap in a single layer of cheesecloth.

5   Place on a rack on a baking sheet and transfer the fish, uncovered, to the refrigerator to dry.

6   Allow the fish to dry for 5 to 7 days, or until it is completely firm.

STORAGE:

The cured fish will keep, refrigerated, for up to 1 week.

BRINED ARTICHOKE HEARTS

Try adding additional herbs or spices to liven up your artichokes. Rosemary, red pepper flakes, and thyme are all excellent choices.

MAKES 2 QUARTS

1½ cups white wine vinegar

9 cups water

30 fresh artichoke hearts

¾ cup fresh lemon juice

4 garlic cloves, smashed

2 tbsp kosher salt

1 tbsp black peppercorns, crushed

2 bay leaves

1   In a large pot, bring the vinegar and 4 cups water to a boil over medium heat. Add the artichoke hearts and simmer for 5 minutes. Drain and let the artichokes cool slightly.

2   Pack the artichokes into prepared quart jars. In a large pot, bring the remaining water, lemon juice, garlic, salt, peppercorns, and bay leaves to a boil.

3   Reduce the heat and let the brine simmer for 5 minutes. Pour the hot brine over the artichokes, leaving ½ inch headspace.

4   Seal the jars and process for 10 to 12 minutes (see page 29). Store in a cool, dark place.

STORAGE:

Processed, these will keep for up to 6 months. Once jars have been opened, store them in the refrigerator, where they will keep for up to 5 days.

BRINED OLIVES

These olives can be flavored with additional herbs, spices, or even garlic or onions, to suit your taste. After curing, they can be packed in oil or left in the brine and used as desired.

MAKES 1 QUART

1½ lb fresh olives

Sprigs of herbs, such as thyme, rosemary, or oregano, as needed (optional)

1 quart (4 cups) Basic Brine (page 136)

2 tbsp olive oil

1 Wash the olives and discard any that are spoiled or bruised. Working in batches, place the olives in a large kitchen towel, cover with another towel, and crack them by rolling a rolling pin over them several times.

2 Transfer the olives to a large bowl, cover in cold water, and refrigerate. Soak them in cold water, changing the water daily, for 1 week.

3 Drain the olives and pack them into a prepared quart jar. If using herbs, place the sprigs in the jar along with the olives. Pour the brine over the olives until the olives are just covered. Pour the olive oil on top.

4 Seal the jar loosely, and transfer the olives to the refrigerator. Let the olives soak in the brine for at least 6 months. The olives can then be used as desired.

STORAGE:

The brined olives will keep, stored in the refrigerator, for up to 3 months.

COUNTRY-STYLE SAUSAGE

Pork fatback can be found in specialty markets and butcher shops. You may have to ask the butcher to reserve the cut if it's not commonly sold.

MAKES ABOUT 5 LB

Casings, as needed

2½ lb pork butt, trimmed of excess fat and diced into 1-inch cubes

1 lb pork fatback, diced into 1-inch cubes (see note)

1 tbsp kosher salt

1 tbsp sugar

2 tsp mustard seed

2 tsp freshly ground white pepper

1¾ tsp Insta Cure No. 1 (page 130)

1½ lb beef shoulder (beef clod), diced into 1-inch cubes

½ cup ice water

1 tbsp paprika

¼ cup nonfat dry milk

1   Prepare the casings (see page 127).

2   Season the pork and pork fat with salt, sugar, mustard seeds, pepper, and Insta Cure. Grind the meat using a ⅜-inch grinding plate, chill, and then grind again through a ¼-inch plate.

3   Grind the beef using a ⅜-inch grinding plate, chill, and then grind again through a ¼-inch plate.

4   Transfer the ground beef and pork mixtures to the bowl of an electric mixer fitted with the paddle attachment. Add the ice water, paprika, and nonfat dry milk, and mix until smooth and sticky.

5   Make and cook a taste-test patty, if desired. Adjust seasoning as desired, and then stuff the mixture into the prepared casings.

6   Prick air pockets into the sausages and tie with string into links about 3 inches long.

7   The sausages can now be stored, smoked, or otherwise cooked.

STORAGE:

The sausages will keep in the refrigerator for up to 5 days or in the freezer for up to 1 month. (Smoked or otherwise cooked, they will keep in the refrigerator for about 3 weeks.)

APPLE CIDER–BRINED TURKEY

Brining the turkey keeps the meat moist and helps it develop better flavor during roasting.

MAKES 1 TURKEY

1 whole turkey (weight of turkey will determine amount of brine used)

1 recipe Apple Cider Brine (page 137)

1 Pump the turkey meat in the thickest areas with 10 percent of its weight in brine.

2 Transfer the pumped turkey to a large container, and cover with the remaining brine. Soak, refrigerated, for 2 days.

3 Remove the turkey from the brine and soak in warm water for 2 hours.

4 Transfer the turkey to a rack set on top of a baking sheet, and place in the refrigerator overnight to allow the pellicle to form (see page 130).

5 Hot smoke the turkey at 185°F until it reaches an internal temperature of 165°F (the total time will depend on the weight of the turkey).

6 Let the turkey rest for 30 minutes before slicing.

VARIATIONS:

APPLE CIDER–BRINED TURKEY BREAST: Replace the whole turkey with turkey breasts. Reduce the brining time to 1 day and the soaking time to 1 hour.

CRANBERRY–APPLE CIDER BRINED TURKEY: Replace the brine with the Cranberry–Apple Cider Brine (page 137).

STORAGE:

The finished turkey will keep, refrigerated, for up to 2 weeks. Frozen, the turkey will keep for up to 6 months.

TASSO

Tasso is a spicy, Cajun-style cured and smoked pork butt. It can be used in soups, sauces, or even as a component of composed dishes.

MAKES ABOUT 4½ LB

5 lb pork butt

4 oz Basic Cure (page 136)

3 tbsp marjoram

2 tbsp freshly ground white pepper

2 tbsp ground allspice

1 tbsp cayenne

1　Cut the pork butt across the grain into slices about 1 inch thick. Press the pork pieces lightly into the dry cure.

2　Cure the pork for 3 hours at room temperature. Rinse the meat in cool water, drain well, and blot dry with paper towels.

3　In a small bowl, combine the marjoram, white pepper, allspice, and cayenne. Dredge the meat in the seasoning on all sides.

4　Air-dry the meat, uncovered in the refrigerator, overnight.

5　Hot smoke the meat at 185°F until the internal temperature registers 155°F, about 2¼ hours.

6　Cool completely, and wrap tightly in plastic wrap.

STORAGE:
The finished ham will keep, refrigerated, for up to 2 weeks.

VENISON SAUSAGE

Pork fatback can be found in specialty markets and butcher shops. You may have to ask the butcher to reserve the cut if it's not commonly sold.

MAKES ABOUT 6 LB

Casings, as needed

5 lb venison, trimmed of excess fat and diced into 1-inch cubes

1 lb pork fatback, diced into 1-inch cubes (see note)

2 tbsp kosher salt

2 tsp freshly ground black pepper

2 tsp dried thyme

1 tbsp lemon zest

½ cup dry white wine

¼ cup nonfat dry milk

1   Prepare the casings (see page 127).

2   Season the venison and pork fat with the salt, pepper, thyme, and lemon zest. Grind the meat using a ¾-inch grinding plate, chill, and then grind again through a ¼-inch plate.

3   Transfer the meat mixture to the bowl of a stand mixer fitted with the paddle attachment. Add the wine and nonfat dry milk and mix until smooth and sticky.

4   Make and cook a taste-test patty, if desired. Adjust the seasoning as desired, and then stuff the mixture into the prepared casings.

5   Prick air pockets into the sausages, and tie with string into links about 4 inches long.

6   The sausages can now be stored, smoked, or otherwise cooked (sautéed, poached, and so on).

STORAGE:

The fresh sausages will keep in the refrigerator for up to 5 days or in the freezer for up to 1 month. (Smoked or otherwise cooked, the sausages will keep in the refrigerator for slightly longer, about 3 weeks.)

BARBECUED BACON

Already delicious and flavorful, bacon is marinated in a sweet and spicy sauce before being hot smoked.

MAKES 5 LB

5 lb pork slab belly

1 cup ketchup

2 tbsp molasses

2 tbsp malt vinegar

1 tbsp Worcestershire sauce

2 tsp Tabasco sauce

½ cup smoked salt

½ cup packed dark brown sugar

¼ cup Spanish paprika

¼ cup dry mustard powder

2 tbsp InstaCure No. 1 (page 130)

1 tbsp freshly ground black pepper

1 tbsp onion powder

2 tsp garlic powder

1   Place the pork slab belly on a large baking sheet. In a medium bowl, whisk together the ketchup, molasses, vinegar, Worcestershire, and Tabasco until fully combined.

2   Brush the marinade onto the pork belly on all sides until fully coated.

3   In a medium bowl, mix together the remaining ingredients to make the cure. Rub the pork with one-quarter of the cure. Cover the pork and refrigerate overnight.

4   Repeat the rubbing and refrigerating process every day for 3 more days until all of the cure has been used. On the fifth day, rub the existing cure into the pork to make sure it is fully absorbed.

5   Rinse the bacon in warm water, and transfer to a cooling rack set on a baking sheet. Allow the bacon to dry in the refrigerator overnight.

6   Hot smoke the bacon at 185°F until it reaches an internal temperature of 155°F.

7   Cool the bacon to room temperature, then transfer to the refrigerator overnight. The bacon can now be sliced and finished as desired.

STORAGE:

The bacon will keep, refrigerated, for up to 1 week. Frozen, the bacon will keep for up to 1 month.

Freezing

Freezing is one of the easiest and most flexible preserving methods—when you're ready to eat something, you simply thaw it and finish it, and then you can replace the space it took up in your freezer with a new item. It is also one of the most effective preserving methods, because it successfully stops spoilage, decay, and bacterial growth, extending the shelf life of most foods to their greatest possible extent.

When you freeze food, all of the moisture in the food is also frozen. Without moisture, bacteria fails to grow, and without warmth, spoilage is brought to a halt, thus preserving food's flavor, texture, and overall quality. However, the quality of frozen food can deteriorate in a number of ways. If frozen for too long, its flavor and texture when thawed will suffer. If food is thawed or partially thawed and then refrozen, its flavor and quality will suffer. In general, food should be kept frozen until ready to used, safely thawed, and then used as soon as possible. Also remember that frozen foods will have the best flavor and texture if frozen at their freshest, so freeze foods within 4 days of purchase.

INGREDIENTS

PRODUCE Most vegetables and fruits freeze well, and freezing preserves their natural colors, flavors, and nutritional value. There are several ways to freeze produce, depending on how you plan on using the food once it is thawed.

* Individually Quick Frozen (IQF) food is the process by which produce and other foods are quickly frozen to keep each piece separate in the packaging. This is ideal for all kinds of produce, both frozen whole (peas, strawberries, green beans) and in pieces (peaches, bell peppers, apples). You can re-create this technique at home (see page 156)
* You can also freeze cooked produce. This is ideal for some foods that don't freeze well raw, like tomatoes. It's also excellent as a method of storing prepared foods: You can freeze jam, fruits in syrup, sauces, and soup bases made from different types of produce.

MEAT, POULTRY, AND FISH Meat, poultry, and fish all freeze very well when properly packaged. They should be removed from the packaging in which they were purchased (with the exception of food that is wrapped in butcher paper), then wrapped tightly in plastic wrap or a tightly sealed plastic bag. If you open a package and use some of the meat and plan to freeze the rest, make sure the remaining meat is tightly wrapped in plastic wrap and then placed in a sealed plastic bag. Meat, poultry, and fish can be frozen in smaller or individual portions to lessen freezing and thawing time. Make sure the meat is completely dry before placing it into the freezer, as excess moisture on the surface will freeze first and can lead to freezer burn (see sidebar, page 165).

RICE AND GRAINS   Cooked rice and other grains freeze well, so freezing is an excellent way to store them if you make too large of a batch. When cooked rice and grains are refrigerated, their moisture allows them to clump up, making their texture suffer when reheated. This allows you only so many options for using the leftover grains. But if you freeze them while it still warm, the grains freeze individually, allowing for more versatile uses later.

BREAD   When properly frozen, bread can keep for up to 3 months in the freezer. Remove the bread from its original packaging and transfer it to a tightly sealed plastic bag. Slicing the bread before freezing makes it easier to remove just the amount you want. A thawed loaf cannot be refrozen, as the quality and texture will completely deteriorate.

CHEESE AND BUTTER   In general, dairy products do not freeze well. There are two exceptions: hard cheeses and butter. Hard cheeses with low moisture, such as Parmesan, can be cut into small blocks (about the size you plan on using) and wrapped tightly in plastic wrap and then in aluminum foil. Be sure to properly thaw them before use. Properly stored, hard cheeses can be frozen for up to 2 months. Butter can be frozen for up to 6 months.

NUTS   Nuts are prone to rancidity and can go stale if not properly stored. They are ideal for freezing, as they freeze and thaw quickly and will keep in the freezer for up to 2 months. You can toast nuts directly from the freezer—just transfer them to a baking sheet or large sauté pan and toast over medium-low heat until they are fragrant.

FLOURS   Many people keep flour in the freezer if they don't use it very frequently, to protect it from bugs and from going rancid. It works especially well for flours that are prone to rancidity, like whole wheat and nut-based flours.

DRIED FOODS   Since dried fruits do not have a long shelf life, they should be frozen if they are not going to be used quickly. For more information on freezing dried foods, see page 95.

FREEZING TECHNIQUES

Following are a variety of techniques that will help you make the most of your freezer. There's one important rule to remember when freezing foods: How will you be using the frozen product? Will you be wanting single-serve portions of frozen vegetables? Will you be

WHAT NOT TO FREEZE

While freezing is an easy and versatile preserving technique, it does not work for everything. The following are some items that do not freeze well:

Celery	Melon
Cucumbers	Milk, Cream, and Yogurt
Green Onions	Radishes
Lettuce	Tomatoes (unless processed)

Some spices also are affected by freezing. Their flavors can become stronger, bitter, and/or overly pungent. Be aware of this when seasoning food that is going to be frozen. When possible, add seasonings to the food after it has been thawed, before it is to be eaten. The following are some spices whose flavors are affected by freezing:

Celery Seed	Onion Powder
Cloves	Paprika
Curry	Pepper
Garlic Powder	

adding several pounds of peaches to a pie filling? Do you like to add a handful of spinach to your pasta? When you freeze foods in the correct size or amount, it makes everything easier. Storage is simpler, and it takes the guesswork out of how much and when to thaw.

GENERAL FREEZING TECHNIQUES

The less time it takes your food to freeze, the less likely it is that ice crystals will form or freezer burn will occur. Therefore, it's best to refrigerate foods until they are very well chilled before you transfer them to the freezer.

Since you will most likely be freezing in large batches, it's wise to make sure that you are freezing food in the quickest, most efficient way. Food freezes faster the smaller and/or flatter it is. Foods placed in plastic bags (prepared soups and sauces, for example) should be placed flat on a baking sheet. They will freeze faster, with less chance of ice crystals forming, and they will take up less storage space. (Quick tip: Place a gallon-size plastic bag inside a medium pot, folding down the sides of the bag over the lip of the pot. This will ease the process of pouring prepared foods into the bag.) For other foods, chose dishes that are wide and flat rather than tall.

It's easiest to freeze casseroles, cakes, loaves, and other foods made in baking and cooking vessels in the containers in which they were made. However, you don't want to tie up all of your favorite dishes in the freezer. Lining the dishes with parchment or freezer paper allows you to freeze the food in the dish, then remove the food, wrap it tightly, and return it to the freezer—without the dish. Remember to leave headspace in the container in which you are freezing the food. This is especially important for food with a high moisture content, because water expands when frozen. In general, 1 inch of headspace is sufficient to ensure that the food does not expand so much that it breaks the container in which it is being held.

INDIVIDUALLY QUICK FREEZING

Individually Quick Frozen (IQF) foods are foods frozen in a single layer so that they remain separate. This technique is easy to re-create in small batches in your own freezer. Keep baking sheets in the freezer until ready to freeze the food. Place the food onto the baking sheet, keeping pieces separate and in a single layer. Freeze food until it's solid — for at least 1 hour. Once the food is fully frozen, transfer it to the proper storage container and label it. This technique works with a variety of foods. You can use foods that are kept whole (such as strawberries or peas), foods that are prepared in some way (halved peaches or diced carrots), and even foods that have been blanched or parcooked (potatoes or greens such as kale or Swiss chard).

MAINTAINING YOUR FREEZER

Your freezer should be defrosted at least once a year, or whenever it accumulates ¼ inch or more of frost). To properly defrost your freezer, remove all foods; they should be held in another freezer, if possible, or in well-iced coolers. Unplug the freezer and open the door. You may want to place large pans and/or towels under the base of the freezer to catch escaping liquid as it defrosts. Once the freezer is fully defrosted, wash and dry the walls and shelves, close the door, and turn the freezer back on. Make sure the freezer is down to the proper temperature before putting the food back inside.

THAWING TECHNIQUES

There are several safe ways to thaw foods. Following are three different thawing methods, along with recommendations for the types of items they will work best for.

In the Refrigerator

Slow, even thawing is easiest in the refrigerator, where the temperature is controlled. Make sure your refrigerator temperature is 40°F or lower. Place items to be thawed on a baking sheet, which will catch any water, juices, or other moisture that melts from the food as it thaws. When thawing foods in the refrigerator, be sure to keep them on a low shelf so that if they do drip or leak, they do not contaminate other foods. While this method is the most recommended, be aware that it is also the most time-consuming; be sure to plan enough time for the food to properly thaw before use. Below is a chart with thawing times for raw food items (thawing time for prepared foods will depend on the quantity and weight of the food).

ITEM	THAWING TIME
Fish	1½ hours per lb
Meat	8 hours per lb
Poultry	4 hours per lb
Produce	4 hours per lb

In Cold Water

This is a fast method of thawing that can reduce the thawing time to 2 hours or less for most foods. Be sure food is in an airtight plastic bag so that it does not come in direct contact with the water or contaminants in the air. Food can be thawed either in a large container or bowl of cold water (70°F or less) or under cold running water. Cold running water is the safest method, because it ensures that the food will slowly thaw at the correct temperature. If you are thawing in a bowl of cold water, be sure to change the water every 30 minutes to ensure the water stays at the proper temperature.

TO THAW OR NOT TO THAW?

Some foods freeze well but don't thaw well. Why would you bother to freeze such items? Because their flavor isn't affected by the freezing process, but rather just their texture. Such foods (including chile peppers, ginger, and fresh herbs) will obviously not be eaten whole or used as a textural component, but they will make great additions to soups, sauces, and marinades. These foods can also be finely chopped and/or made into a paste and stored in ice cube trays (about 1 tablespoon of paste per cube), making them easy to add to dishes later.

EQUIPMENT

While freezing is an extremely simple and economical form of preserving, it does require some investment in the proper equipment. Once you have the correct tools, freezing will be even easier.

FREEZERS The good thing about freezers is that most people already have one. The tips and techniques in this chapter can be used for small freezers, such as the ones attached to kitchen refrigerators. However, if you plan on freezing large quantities or a huge variety of items, you may want to invest in an additional or larger freezer (see Resources, page 172). Such freezers come in all shapes and sizes—chest freezers are usually short and wide, whereas reach-in freezers are tall and resemble most standard refrigerators. Choose whichever works for you and your storage space, but here are some things to look out for when choosing a freezer:

* Temperature capabilities: The most ideal freezing temperature is below 0°F. Many freezers do not have the capability to reach and/ or stay at that temperature.
* Energy efficiency: Since your freezer will be running year-round, you may want to choose one that is particularly energy efficient. Most models boast at least some levels of efficiency, but take a careful look at each model you are considering.

* Size: A big freezer is ideal if you plan on preserving large quantities of food. However, it is important to be realistic. If you choose a large freezer and cannot fully stock it, it won't run efficiently and the food you do store could suffer. Likewise, you do not want to choose a small freezer and then run out of freezer space before the summer preserving season is over.

CONTAINERS AND PACKAGING   As with any preserving method, it's important to have the right containers—and lots of them. In general, wide, shallow containers work best. as they promote quick and efficient freezing. Choose containers with airtight seals made from food-safe materials. Glass and plastic are the two most preferred container materials, but be sure that you choose containers that specify that they are freezer safe.

Plastic bags are excellent for use in freezing, but choose bags specifically meant for freezer use with a seal that is airtight and easy to use. Once the food is placed inside, force as much air out as possible before sealing the bag. Vacuum-sealed bags are wonderful for freezing, because they remove all air from the bag and form a completely airtight seal (see Resources, page 172).

Plastic wrap and aluminum foil are good for providing an extra layer of protection between the food and the outside air. Wrap the food once or twice and then place it into an airtight plastic bag. Freezer paper is excellent for a first layer of wrapping for food. It's especially good for meat, poultry, and fish.

VERTICAL COOLING RACKS AND BAKING SHEETS   This is the most recommended equipment for the Individually Quick Frozen method (see page 156). Food can be placed onto baking sheets and stored on the racks. You do not need the vertical rack, but if your freezer has the space for it, it will allow you to freeze multiple items at any given time without having to leave space in the freezer empty or balance the baking sheets on other food. Use good-quality, heavy baking sheets made of food-safe materials (especially if food is to be placed directly on the baking sheets, in which case you should not use sheets with nonstick coating). Vertical, multi-sheet cooling racks can generally be found with other baking items in your local kitchen supply store.

How Long Can I Freeze It?

TYPE OF FOOD	MONTHS FROZEN
Ground meat	3
Steaks, chops, cutlets, etc.	9
Roasts	12
Sausages	3
Bacon	1
Ham	2
Poultry	12 (whole), 6 (parts)
Fish	4–6
Seafood	3
Vegetables	8
Fruits	8
Bread and rolls	3
Muffins and quick breads	3
Cakes	3
Cookies	6
Soups and stews	5
Purees and sauces	4
Prepared dishes	5

HOW TO ORGANIZE
YOUR FREEZER

Organization will vary from person to person, but it's important to re-member that space in your freezer is valuable and you should make the most of it. Here are a few tips and tricks to make your freezer more organized and efficient:

* Keep meat, fish, and poultry as near to the bottom as possible, as that area tends to be the coldest part of the freezer with the least amount of temperature variance.

* Set up racks to increase space efficiency. Some freezers have adjustable shelves, but for those that don't, inexpensive wire or metal racks are ideal for increasing your space and making your freezer more organized. Cabinet organizers are also ideal since they are made to fit in nooks and crannies. A multi-tiered cool-ing rack is great to use for quick-freezing items (see page 156) or for freezing prepared foods like cakes, pies, soups, or casseroles before they go to their final storage area.

* Choose containers that will store easily. Containers that stack are wonderful because they allow you to maximize space, whereas oddly shaped containers can take up more space than necessary. Taller containers are ideal for reach-in freezers, because they fit easily into door compartments.

* Label everything. Once food goes into the freezer it can be easy to forget what it is, especially if it's properly wrapped. Label each container or package with its contents and the date it was placed into the freezer. It's also a good idea to label different compart-ments and areas of your freezer. This ensures that all similar items stay together, making them easier to find and making it easier to see when you're beginning to run low. You can also keep track of amounts of food on the freezer door (on a dry-erase board, bulletin board, or handwritten list) so that you can see what is available before you open the door.

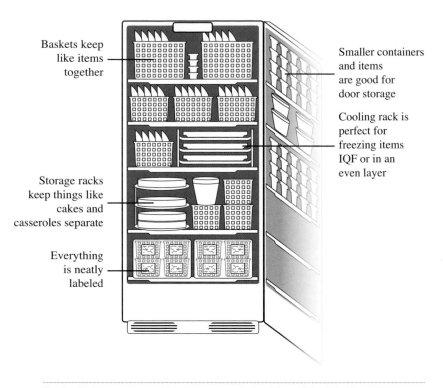

Baskets keep like items together

Smaller containers and items are good for door storage

Cooling rack is perfect for freezing items IQF or in an even layer

Storage racks keep things like cakes and casseroles separate

Everything is neatly labeled

Keeping like items together and labeled is even easier by adding additional shelving or bins to your reach-in freezer.

How to Freeze Safely

Freezing is a very effective method of preserving food, but as with any preservation method, there are some safety concerns.

TEMPERATURE DANGER ZONE

It is very important to be aware of the temperature danger zone when freezing. When you cook hot foods that you intend to freeze, it is important to cool them properly before placing them into the freezer. Soup, for example, cannot go directly from the pot to the freezer.

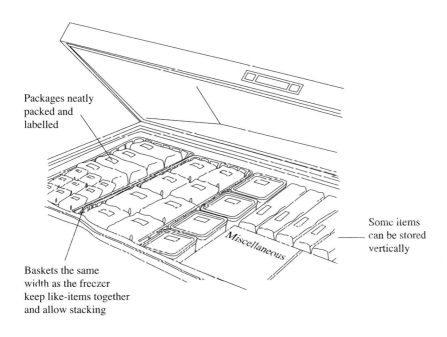

Packages neatly packed and labelled

Some items can be stored vertically

Baskets the same width as the freezer keep like-items together and allow stacking

Chest freezers can be more difficult to keep organized because everything cannot be kept in direct sight. Keep more frequently used items near the surface, where they are easier to reach, and store them in moveable bins so that reaching the base of the freezer is a snap.

KEEPING THE CORRECT TEMPERATURE AND HUMIDITY

Freezers operate most effectively when they are full (not overly full or stuffed, but with items in each area of the freezer and on each shelf). If your supply of frozen foods is diminishing and you have nothing to replenish it, place some water in open containers in the freezer. This will keep the freezer temperature from overly fluctuating due to lack of food inside. It can also help to maintain proper humidity levels.

Some items can be cooled gently over an ice bath. Others can be cooled to room temperature, then transferred to the refrigerator to chill slightly prior to freezing. Consider refrigerating raw items, like fruits, vegetables, and nuts, before freezing. If the foods are already chilled, it will reduce the amount of time they spend in the danger zone before becoming properly frozen.

THAWING AND CROSS CONTAMINATION

Proper thawing is vitally important prior to the use of frozen foods. There are two main health concerns related to thawing. Once thawed, most foods will begin to rapidly decline in quality and are more prone to spoilage. Unless directed otherwise, use thawed foods within 24 hours. Also be aware of the potential for cross con-tamination when thawing. Place thawing foods on a baking sheet, which will catch any juices or moisture released from the food as it thaws. If thawing in the refrigerator, be sure to place thawing foods on a low shelf so that the food does not drip or leak over onto any other foods.

BACTERIA AND OTHER CAUSES OF FOOD-BORNE ILLNESSES

Freezing stops the growth of bacteria by freezing the moisture in food and keeping it in a properly chilled state. However, freezing does not destroy bacteria and other causes of food-borne illnesses, and once food is thawed, such harmful factors may be present. Be aware of this, and take regular precautions to properly thaw and store food until ready to cook. Cook food to the proper doneness to ensure that any traces of bacteria are killed before the food is pack-aged, stored, and/or consumed.

FREEZER BURN

Freezer burn occurs when air reaches frozen food. This causes oxidation (which can cause changes in color) and dehydration (which can affect texture, flavor, and overall quality when thawed). While freezer burn reduces the overall quality of the food, it is not a food safety risk. Exposure to air does not change the fact the food is properly chilled, and it will not be a source of bacteria or spoilage. There are several ways to protect against freezer burn:

* Store foods to be frozen properly in airtight containers. If food is not stored properly (if a seal is broken or not properly formed), air will get to the food, and it will eventually develop freezer burn. Wrap foods tightly and/or be sure that seals are fully formed before transferring food to the freezer.

* Reduce the temperature variance in your freezer. Open your freezer as little as possible, and don't keep it open for extended periods of time. Fluctuations in temperature can cause moisture to melt slightly and/or to rise to the surface of food, where it can evaporate, causing the food to become dehydrated and develop freezer burn.

MAKING YOUR OWN PANTRY STAPLES

As mentioned throughout this book, preserving is a
wonderful way to eat fresh, healthy foods, save money,
and savor seasonality. This chapter includes a variety of
delicious recipes to add to your pantry, as well as some
handy guidelines for how to organize it.

PANTRY SETUP
AND ORGANIZATION

A clean and organized pantry can completely alter the way you cook. A properly stocked pantry means you can make many recipes simply with what you have on hand, which eliminates last-minute grocery runs. In addition, a well-organized pantry makes it easy to see what you have, what needs to be replenished, and what needs to be used up before it goes bad. If executed properly, you can reduce or eliminate food waste and make the most of all of your ingredients. Here are some important factors to keep in mind when organizing your pantry.

* Keep the pantry cool, dark, and dry. Many foods are adversely affected by light, and moisture and/or heat can promote spoilage, bacterial growth, and even the presence of pests.

* Invest in plenty of containers. Transfer typical pantry items to their own airtight containers to prevent the piling up of open packages of pasta, dried beans, or other ingredients. Glass is great because it's nonporous and clear, but metal and plastic work equally well.

* Make sure everything is visible. Keep items in neat configurations so you can easily see what you have. If your cabinets or shelves are particularly deep, store items that are the same in rows going toward the back of the cabinet, keeping the oldest product toward the front for immediate use. If your shelves have lots of space between them vertically, you may want to purchase additional shelving or shelf expanders that will allow you to store multiple items vertically without stacking them.

* Label everything clearly. Label cans, jars, and other containers with the date they were stored in the pantry, the date they were opened, and/or the date they need to be used by. While this is especially important for homemade foods, it can be handy for purchased items as well, so that you can easily see when items were purchased or initially opened.

* Decide on an organization system. When it comes to organization, no one can decide what is best but you—you're the one who will be using the kitchen and the ingredients on a daily basis. Whatever system you choose, follow and maintain it. Here are a few suggestions for organizing your pantry:

STORE BY SEASON OR BY DATE MADE/PURCHASED: Store items that were made during summer or with summer produce together. Alternatively, keep items that need to be used quickly in the same space and items for longer-term storage in a different area.

ORGANIZE BY USE: Store similar items together or near each other. This can be interpreted in a myriad of ways:

- dried pasta and tomato sauce
- cocoa powder, chocolate bars, and chocolate chips
- flour, sugar, and baking powder

STORE BY METHOD: Store dried items together (dried herbs, chiles, garlic, pasta, and so forth), store canned items together (jams, jellies, pickles, and so on.

＊ Keep a master list. Hang a dry-erase board or bulletin board, and keep track of when large quantities of items go in and when they need to go out.

＊ Check everything occasionally. Despite your best efforts, some open items might be forgotten or pushed to the back, so check your shelves every now and then for anything that is in the wrong place, past its prime, or spoiled.

＊ Keep it clean. Beyond being organized, your pantry will be at its fullest potential when it's clean. Keep shelves free of dust and food particles, and keep items off of the floor, where they are more likely to become contaminated. Keep cleaning supplies and other non-food items in a separate area.

One way to organize your pantry is by grouping similar items together for ease of use.

Organize your canned goods by season, and keep older jars near the front so that they'll be used up first.

Other items may be stored in the pantry (such as storage containers and cleaning supplies), but remember to keep them separate from ready-to-eat products.

APPLE BUTTER

✖ ✖

You can use a variety of apples for this apple butter, but a mixture of tart and sweet apples works best. Try Granny Smith, McIntosh, Gala, and Jonathans.

MAKES 3 PINTS

5 lb apples, peeled, cored, and diced

1¾ cups apple cider

1¼ cups sugar

2 tbsp fresh lemon juice

Pinch of kosher salt

1   In a large pot, bring the apples and cider to a boil over medium high heat, stirring occasionally to prevent sticking or burning.

2   Reduce the heat to low, and simmer until the apples are soft, 30 to 35 minutes. Use a potato masher, fork, or immersion blender to coarsely mash the mixture.

3   Stir in the sugar, lemon juice, and salt.

4   Continue to simmer until the liquid has evaporated and the mixture is thick, 40 to 50 minutes more. The mixture will be relatively smooth but may have a few chunks — for a completely smooth butter, you may want to puree it lightly at this point in a blender or with a handheld immersion blender.

5   Pour the finished apple butter into prepared pint jars, leaving ¼ inch of headspace. Seal the jars, and process for 7 to 10 minutes. Store in a cool, dark place.

VARIATIONS:

PUMPKIN BUTTER: Replace the apples with peeled, seeded, and diced pumpkin. Increase the initial cooking time to 35 to 40 minutes, or until the pumpkin is tender. Replace ¼ cup of the sugar with ¼ cup packed brown sugar, and add 1 tsp ground ginger along with the salt.

SPICED APPLE BUTTER: Add 2 tsp ground cinnamon and a pinch of ground nutmeg and cloves.

STORAGE:

Processed, this apple butter will keep for up to 6 months. Once jars have been opened, store them in the refrigerator, where they will keep for up to 1 week.

PICKLING SPICE

As with many of the recipes in this book, this can be tweaked to suit your tastes, but our base recipe includes the standard flavors that make for one delicious pickling brine.

MAKES ABOUT 1 CUP

⅓ cup mustard seed, crushed

3 tbsp allspice berries, crushed

2 tbsp coriander seed, crushed

2 tbsp black peppercorns, crushed

1 tbsp dill seed, crushed

1 tbsp ground ginger

1 tsp ground mace

5 cloves, crushed

2 bay leaves, crumbled

1 cinnamon stick, coarsely chopped

Combine all of the ingredients. The spices should still be in large pieces, but crushed enough so that their flavors and aromas will release when added to a recipe.

STORAGE:

The spice mix will keep in an airtight container for up to 2 months.

RESOURCES

ONLINE RESOURCES

Find a Farmer's Market, Farm Stand, Co-op, or CSA
http://www.localharvest.org

National Center for Home Food Preservation
http://www.uga.edu/nchfp

General Preservation Information
http://www.preservefood.com

Canning Supplies
http://www.canningpantry.com
http://www.freshpreserving.com

Dehydrating Supplies
http://www.nesco.com/
http://www.canningpantry.com/dehydrators.html

Brining, Curing, and Smoking Supplies
www.butcher-packer.com
www.sausagemaker.com

Freezing Supplies
http://www.homedepot.com/webapp/wcs/stores/servlet/
ContentView?pn=Refrigerators_Freezers&langId=-1&storeId=10
051&catalogId=10053

PRINT RESOURCES

Alltrista Consumer Products. *Ball Blue Book Guide to Preserving.*
2004.
Stoner, Carol Hupping, ed. *Stocking Up: How to Preserve the Foods
You Grow, Naturally.* 1977.
U.S. Department of Agriculture. *Complete Guide to Home Canning
and Preserving.* 2009.

INDEX

Page numbers in *italics* indicate illustrations

RENO PUBLIC LIBRARY

DISCARD

1.6.14